8

Scott Foresman

Accelerating English Language Learning

Authors

Anna Uhl Chamot

Jim Cummins

Carolyn Kessler

J. Michael O'Malley

Lily Wong Fillmore

Consultant

George González

Longman

Illustrations Unless otherwise acknowledged, all illustrations are the property of Scott, Foresman and Company. Page abbreviations are as follows: (T) top, (B) bottom, (L) left, (R) right, (C) center.

Deborah Wolfe/Skip Baker 43, 46(B)–47(R); Shawn Banner 12(T), 26–37, 180(C)–181(B,R); Clare Jett/Jennifer Bolton 128, 214; Melissa Turk/Ka Botzis 83(T); Edward Burton 90, 101, 194–195(B); Deborah Wolfe/Anthony Cericola 87(TR); Ebet Dudley 16(TL), 19(R), 20(TL); American Artists/Lane Dupont 13(L), 38; Allan Eitzen 126–127, 199(T), 228; Cornell & McCarthy/Doris Ettlinger 154–155(BC); Bill Farnsworth 164–171; Howard S. Friedman 120(B); Laurie Harden 76; American Artists/Doug Henry 114; Richard Salzman/Denise Hilton-Campbell 14, 48-49, 157; Dilys Evans/Laura Kelly 10(T), 138-139; Mattleson Associates/Karen Kluglein 8–9, 22(B)–23(T); Bob Lange 24(L), 68(T), 118–119, 125(T), 130–131, 189; Gayle Levee 50–57; Carol Chislovsky/David Lund 216–217, 224-225; Carol Chislovsky/Peg Magovern 183; Mapping Specialists 70–71, 80, 86(T), 156(B), 159(T), 185(T), 188(R); Carol Chislovsky/Paul Mirocha 190; Square Moon/Elizabeth Morales 17(T), 21, 25(TR); Deborah Wolfe/Andy Myer 152; Deborah Wolfe/Saul Rosenbaum 94(T), 100(T); Carla Simmons 163; Holly Hahn/Steve Snodgrass 206–213; Richard Salzman/Wayne Anthony Still 156(T); Carol Chislovsky/Cathy Trachok 160(T), 174(R)–177(B), 200–201; Christina Tugeau/Meryl Treatner 4(L)-5(R), 12(R); Elaine Wadsworth 10–11, 75; Elizabeth Wolf 58, 63(B), 72(T), 73(T), 74, 172.

Literature 26–37: From LITTLE BROTHER OF THE WILDERNESS by Meridel Le Sueur. Copyright © 1947 by Meridel LeSueur. Reprinted by permission of Alfred A. Knopf, Inc. 50–57: "Why the Monsoon Comes Each Year" reprinted by permission of G. P. Putnam's Sons from FAIRY TALES FROM VIET NAM, retold by Dorothy Lewis Robertson. Copyright © 1968 by Dorothy Lewis Robertson. 102–113: From THUNDER AT GETTYSBURG by Patricia Lee Gauch. Copyright © 1975 by Patricia Lee Gauch, illustrations copyright © 1975 by Stephen Gammell. Reprinted by permission of G. P. Putnam's Sons. 140–147: From THE SOLAR SYSTEM by Maura Gouck. Copyright © 1993 by The Child's World, Inc. Reprinted by permission. 164–171: From SARAH, PLAIN AND TALL by Patricia MacLachlan. Copyright © 1985 by Patricia MacLachlan. Reprinted by permission of HarperCollins. 184–187: Reprinted with the permission of Atheneum Books for Young Readers, an imprint of Simon & Schuster from GREAT LIVES: HUMAN RIGHTS by William Jay Jacobs. Copyright © 1990 by William Jay Jacobs. 206–213: From LETTERS FROM RIFKA by Karen Hesse. Copyright © 1992 by Karen Hesse. Reprinted by permission of Henry Holt and Co., Inc.

Poems and Songs 14: "Turn! Turn! Turn! (To Everything There Is a Season)" words from the Book of Ecclesiastes, adaptation and music by Pete Seeger. TRO © Copyright 1962 (Renewed) Melody Trails, Inc., New York, NY. Used by permission. 58: "Lotsa Winds" from CRACKERS AND CRUMBS by Sonja Dunn. Copyright © 1990 by Sonja Dunn and Lou Pamenter. Reprinted with permission of Pembroke Publishers Limited. 75: "Raindrop" from THERE'S MOTION EVERYWHERE by John Travers Moore. Copyright © 1970 by John Travers Moore. Reprinted by permission. 76: "Good Day Sunshine" words and music by John Lennon and Paul McCartney. Copyright © 1966. Used by permission. 126–127: "Here Comes the Sun" words and music by George Harrison. Copyright © 1969, 1981. Used by permission. 128: "Brazilian Moon Tale" by Jane Yolen reprinted bypermission of Philomel Books from WHAT RHYMES WITH MOON? text copyright © 1993 by Jane Yolen, illustrations copyright © 1993 by Ruth Tietjen Councell. 190: "Brother, Can You Spare a Dime?" by E. Y. Harburg and Jay Gorney. Copyright ©1932 (Renewed) Warner Bros. Inc. Rights for extended renewal term in U.S. controlled by Glocca Morra Music and Gorney Music Publishers. Canadian rights controlled by Warner Bros. Inc. All rights reserved. Used by permission of Warner Bros. Publications US Inc., Miami, FL 33014. 214: ALL Reference to "God Bless America" THERE SHOULD BE NO PERMISSION FOR THIS PAGE. 228: "Hang Out the Flags" by James S. Tippett.

ISBN: 0-13-027501-8

Copyright © 2001, 1997 Scott, Foresman and Company
All Rights Reserved. Printed in the United States of America.

Photography Unless otherwise acknowledged, all photographs are the property of Scott, Foresman and Company. Page abbreviations are as follows: (T) top, (C) center, (B) bottom, (R) right.

v (t) Erich Lessing/Art Resource, (br) TSADO/NASA/Tom Stack & Associates; 2(t), 3(tl, tr, b) Superstock, Inc.; 8 Courtesy U.S.D.A; 12 UPI/Corbis-Bettmann; 13(c) Focus on Sports, Inc.; (t) REUTERS/Jean Paul Pelissier/Archive Photos; 16, 17(b) Superstock, Inc.; (t) Jim Strawser/Grant Heilman Photography; 18 Larry LeFever/Grant Heilman Photography; 19 Runk/Schoenberger/Grant Heilman Photography; 20, 22, 23, 25(t, b), 39(t, b), 40–41, 40(t) Superstock, Inc.; (bl) NSSL/NOAA; 41(b) Grant Heilman/Grant Heilman Photography; 41(t) Holt Confer/Grant Heilman Photography; (c) Arthur C. Smith III/Grant Heilman Photography; 42(c, r) Superstock, Inc.; (l) NASA; 46–47 Superstock, Inc.; 59(b) NSSL/NOAA; (r) Grant Heilman/Grant Heilman Photography; 60(b) Superstock, Inc.; 60-61(background) NASA; 61(b) © CNES 1988; 65(b) NASA; 66(t) James Deeton/Tony Stone Images; (c, b), 70(t), 71(b), 72 Superstock, Inc.; 77 NASA; 78–79(background), 78(inset) North Wind Picture Archives; 79(t, br-insets) Granger Collection, New York; (bl-inset) Collection of Mr. William S. Powell; 80(c) Brown Brothers; 81, 82(b) North Wind Picture Archives; 82(t) Brown Brothers; 83(b) Southern Historical Collection CB#3926, Wilson Library, The University of North Carolina at Chapel Hill ; (t) Library of Congress; 84(cl) North Wind Picture Archives; 84(t, b, cr), 85(t, bl, br) Granger Collection, New York; (c) North Wind Picture Archives; 86–87, 88 Granger Collection, New York; 89(t, b) Sophia Smith Collection, Smith College; 91 Library of Congress; 92 Granger Collection, New York; 93(t) Library of Congress; 93(b), 94–95 Granger Collection, New York; 95(t) Library of Congress; 96(b) Superstock, Inc.; (t) Granger Collection, New York; 97(b) Jack Novak/Photri, Inc.; (t) Granger Collection, New York; 98(r) U.S. Signal Corps Photo, National Archives, Brady Collection; (l) Granger Collection, New York; 99(b) Library of Congress; (t) Brown Brothers; 115(b) Library of Congress; (t, c) Granger Collection, New York; 116(b) Steven Hunt/Image Bank; (t) TSADO/NASA/Tom Stack & Associates; 117(b) NASA/JPL/TSADO/Tom Stack & Associates; (t) Superstock, Inc.; (c) NASA/Airworks/Tom Stack & Associates; 118–119(background) Bill & Sally Fletcher/Tom Stack & Associates; 120–121 Superstock, Inc.; 120(t) NASA/Tom Stack & Associates; 123 Bill & Sally Fletcher/Tom Stack & Associates; 124(t) Egyptian National Museum, Cairo/Superstock, Inc., (bl) Erich Lessing/Art Resource, (br) Pollak/Art Resource; 125(b) Erich Lessing/Art Resource; 129(b) TSADO/NASA/Tom Stack & Associates; Bill & Sally Fletcher/Tom Stack & Associates; 130–131 Photri; 130(t, b), 131(t) NASA; (c) NASA/JPL/TSADO/Tom Stack & Associates; 132 JPL/TSADO/Tom Stack & Associates; 133(b) USGS/TSADO/Tom Stack & Associates; (c) NASA; (t) NASA/TSADO/Tom Stack & Associates; 134(t) NASA/ESA/Tom Stack & Associates; (c) Photri; (t) Superstock, Inc.; 135(t, b) JPL/NASA; 136(b) Corbis-Bettmann; (tr) NASA; (tl) Photri; 137(br) NASA; (bl) JPL/Tom Stack & Associates; (tr) Photri; (tl) NASA; 140 JPL/TSADO/Tom Stack & Associates; 141(inset) Superstock, Inc.; (background) Mike O'Brine/Tom Stack & Associates; 142 Photri; 143 JPL/TSADO/Tom Stack & Associates; 144 NASA/JPL/Tom Stack & Associates; 145(l) Superstock, Inc.; (r) NASA; (background) Mike O'Brine/Tom Stack & Associates; 146 Photri; 147 NASA/Airworks/Tom Stack & Associates; 148 NASA; 149(r) Corbis-Bettmann; (l) NASA; 150(b) JPL/Superstock, Inc.; (t) Corbis-Bettmann; 151(b) JPL/Photri; (t) Corbis-Bettmann; 153(t, b) NASA; (background) Bill & Sally Fletcher/Tom Stack & Associates; 154 Granger Collection, New York; 155(b) Stock Montage, Inc.; (c) Superstock, Inc.; 158(t, b) Granger Collection, New York; 159(b) Gary Irving/Tony Stone Images; 159(t), 160, 161, 162(b) Granger Collection, New York; 162(t) James P. Rowan/Tony Stone Images; 173, 174–175(c), 174(b) Granger Collection, New York; (t) Superstock, Inc.; 175(tr, b), 176(b) Granger Collection, New York; (t) North Wind Picture Archives; 177(b) Granger Collection, New York; (t) Corbis-Bettmann Archive; 178(b) Stock Montage, Inc.; (t, c) Corbis-Bettmann; 179(b) Superstock, Inc.; 179(tl, tr), 180(t, b) Granger Collection, New York; 181 Stock Montage, Inc.; 184 Culver Pictures Inc.; 185, 186(t) Granger Collection, New York; (b) National Archives; 187(b) Superstock, Inc.; (t) Library of Congress; (c) Carnegie Hero Fund Commission; 188, 189 Granger Collection, New York; 190 UPI/Corbis-Bettmann; 191(b) Granger Collection, New York; (tl, tr) Superstock, Inc.; 192–193 Mark Richards/PhotoEdit; (br) Bob Daemmrich; (br) F. Lee Corkran/Sygma; 192(t) Corbis-Bettmann Archive; 193(t) Superstock, Inc.; (b) Sophia Smith Collection; (c) David R. Frazier; 195 John Neubaugh/PhotoEdit; 196–197(b) 1995 Dennis Brack/Black Star; 196(t) UPI/Corbis-Bettmann; 198(t) Willie L. Hill Jr./Stock Boston; (b) Billy E. Barnes/ PhotoEdit; 199 Ben Van Hook/Black Star; 202(t, b) Superstock, Inc.; 203(b) Koni Nordmann/Focus/Matrix International, Inc.; (t) Corbis-Bettmann Archive; 204(b) 1988 Andrew Popper/Popperfoto; 204–205(b) Jacob Riis Collection, Museum of the City of New York; 205(b) ©1988 Andrew Popper/Popperfoto; 217(b) UPI/Corbis-Bettmann; 218 U.S. Capitol Historical Society/National Geographic Photographer George F. Mobley; 219 Paul Conklin/PhotoEdit; 220(t) Superstock, Inc.; (b) Paul Conklin/PhotoEdit; 221 95 Dennis Brack/Black Star; 222 Superstock, Inc.; 223 Sygma; 226 ©1995 Tribune Media Services, Inc. All rights Reserved.; 227(b) Superstock, Inc.

Sandra H. Bible
Elementary ESL Teacher
Shawnee Mission School District
Shawnee Mission, Kansas

Anaida Colón-Muñiz, Ed.D.
Director of English Language
Development
and Bilingual Education
Santa Ana Unified School District
Santa Ana, California

Debbie Corkey-Corber
Educational Consultant
Williamsburg, Virginia

Barbara Crandall
Carol Baranyi
Ilean Zamlut
ESOL Teachers
Lake Park Elementary School
Palm Beach County, Florida

Lily Pham Dam
Instructional Specialist
Dallas Independent School District
Dallas, Texas

María Delgado
Milwaukee Public Schools
Milwaukee, Wisconsin

Dr. M. Viramontes de Marín
Chair, Department of Education and
Liberal Studies at the National
Hispanic University
San Jose, California

Virginia Hansen
ESOL Resource Teacher
Palm Beach County, Florida

Tim Hart
Supervisor of English as a Second
Language
Wake County
Releigh, North Carolina

Lilian I. Jezik
Bilingual Resource Teacher
Corona-Norco Unified School District
Norco, California

Helen L. Lin
Chairman, Education Program
Multicultural Arts Council of
Orange County, California
Formerly ESL Lab Director,
Kansas City, Kansas Schools

Justine McDonough
Trish Lirio
Sheree Di Donato
Jupiter Elementary School
West Palm Beach, Florida

Teresa Montaña
United Teachers Los Angeles
Los Angeles, California

Loriana M. Novoa, Ed.D.
Research and Evaluation Consultants
Miami, Florida

Beatrice Palls
ESOL and Foreign Language
Supervisor
Pasco County, Florida

Rosa María Peña
Austin Independent School District
Austin, Texas

Alice Quarles
Assistant Principal
Fairlawn Elementary School
Dade County, Florida

Thuy Pham-Remmele
ESL/Bilingual K–12 Specialist
Madison Metropolitan School District
Madison, Wisconsin

Jacqueline J. Servi Margis
ESL and Foreign Language
Curriculum Specialist
Milwaukee Public Schools
Milwaukee, Wisconsin

Carmen Sorondo
Supervisor, ESOL, K–12
Hillsborough County, Florida

Susan C. VanLeuven
Poudre R-1 School District
Fort Collins, Colorado

Rosaura Villaseñor
(Educator)
Norwalk, California

Cheryl Wilkinson
J. O. Davis Elementary School
Irving Independent School District
Irving, Texas

Phyllis I. Ziegler
ESL/Bilingual Consultant
New York, New York

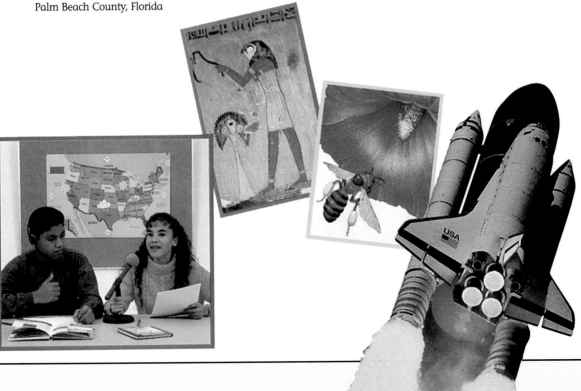

TABLE OF CONTENTS

Cycles of Life

Word Bank

body shape

eye color

hair color

height

weight

Tell what you know.

How are the people in a family alike?

How do people change over the years?

Talk About It

Do you have brothers or sisters? In what ways do you look alike?

3

CHAPTER 1

Growing Up

How We Grow

When girls are between 9 and 13 years old, they have a growth spurt. Boys have their growth spurt when they are between 11 and 15 years old. For example, a 14-year-old boy might grow 4 inches (10 centimeters) in one year.

Growth Spurt in Girls
The growth spurt usually begins earlier in girls than in boys.
Girls gain the most weight about the age of 12 or 13.
Girls reach their adult height about the age of 18.

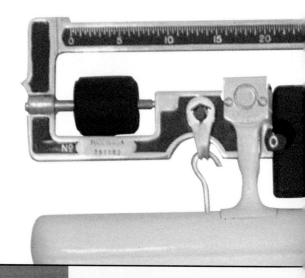

At these ages, young people's bodies suddenly grow more quickly. Their feet and hands get bigger. Their arms and legs get longer. But other parts of their bodies do not grow as fast.

The different rates of growth cause some problems. Many young people feel awkward when they move. But soon the other parts of their bodies grow too. The young people begin to lose their awkwardness.

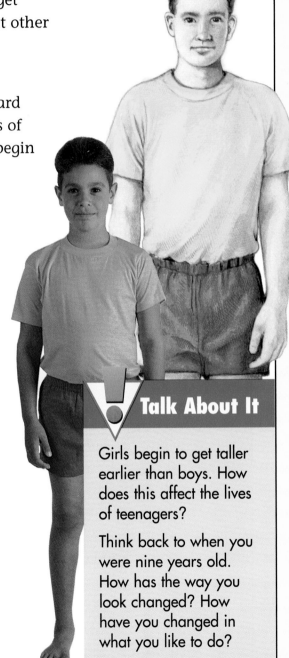

Growth Spurt in Boys

The growth spurt usually begins later in boys than in girls.
Boys gain the most weight about the age of 14 or 15.
Boys reach their adult height about the age of 20.

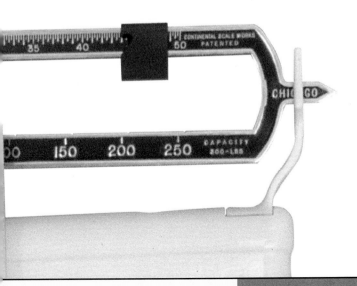

Talk About It

Girls begin to get taller earlier than boys. How does this affect the lives of teenagers?

Think back to when you were nine years old. How has the way you look changed? How have you changed in what you like to do?

Heredity and Growth

You have certain **traits.** Traits include your height, hair color, and eye color. They also include the ages at which your growth spurt begins and ends. You get your traits from your parents. The passing of traits from parents to children is called **heredity.**

Traits are passed from parents to children in **genes.** Genes make you look like your parents. You get half your genes from your mother and half from your father. This mixture of genes determines your traits. For example, if your parents are tall, you probably will be tall. Your parents will pass on to you their trait for tallness.

Great-Grandparents

← **Grandparents** →

← **Parents** →

Father

Mother

Veronica

Look at the family tree. Notice how some of Veronica's parents, grandparents, and great-grandparents were tall. They passed on the trait for tallness to her.

Talk About It

How are genes and growth related?

What traits do you share with your family?

Food and Growth

In order to grow well, you need to eat the right kinds of foods. You also need to eat the right amounts of them. The Food Pyramid shows the right kinds of foods and the amounts you should eat.

To stay healthy, you need to eat foods from the bottom five groups. You should avoid foods from the top group.

Fats, oils, sweets

A serving equals one tablespoon of butter. Use sparingly.

Dairy Products: Milk, yogurt, and cheese

A serving equals one cup of milk or 2 ounces of cheese. Eat 2–3 servings a day.

Meat, poultry, fish, dry beans, eggs, and nuts

A serving equals two eggs or 3 ounces of cooked meat. Eat 2–3 servings a day.

Vegetables

A serving equals one potato or one half cup of carrots. Eat 3–5 servings a day.

Fruit

A serving equals one apple or one half cup of grapes. Eat 2–4 servings a day.

Write About It

Look at the food groups again. What are your favorite foods from each group? What do you like to eat for a healthful snack?

Grains: Bread, cereal, rice, and pasta

A serving equals one slice of bread or one ounce of cereal. Eat 6–11 servings a day.

Word Bank

eggs

fish

orange juice

potatoes

rice

strawberries

toast

tortillas

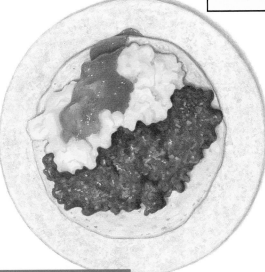

Try It Out

Look at the different breakfasts. What food groups do they include? Talk with a partner, and decide what you would choose for a healthful breakfast. Then decide on healthful meals for lunch and supper.

How big is a foot?

Long ago, people did not use rulers. They measured how long things were by using parts of their bodies, such as their feet. But there was a problem. Everyone's foot was a different length.

In 1324, King Edward II of England made a law. The law said a "foot" would always be the same length. People could then be sure how long something was. When people bought a foot of cloth, it was always the same length.

![Talk About It]

Why do people use the same units of measurement? What units of measurement are used in the United States? What other units of measurement do you know?

What would happen if everybody used his or her own feet for measuring? The same object would have different lengths depending on whose foot is used for measuring. Imagine buying a foot of ribbon. If it costs 75 cents for each foot, you might want to use your father's foot instead of yours!

Measuring with Our Feet		
How Many Feet Long Is . . . ?	Using My Feet	Using My Partner's Feet
The Teacher's Desk		
The Longest Classroom Wall		
A Hall in My School		
The Playground or Athletic Field		

Try It Out

Work with a partner to measure things. Place the heel of one foot directly in front of the toes of the other foot. Count each step as a "foot." Are your numbers different from those of your partner?

Fun Facts

People like to measure things and keep records. Here are some interesting facts about people. They are from *The Guinness Book of Records*.

The Longest Feet

Matthew McGrory from the state of Pennsylvania has the longest feet. He wears size 23 shoes. His shoes are about 15 inches (40 centimeters) long. How much longer is his foot than yours?

The Longest Hair

Diane Witt has the longest hair in the United States. In 1993, her hair was more than 12 feet 8 inches (3 meters 86 centimeters) long. Usually hair grows only up to 3 feet (1 meter) long.

The Oldest Family

Do you know your great-great-great-grandparents? A family in China can name members of its family back to 2,800 years ago.

Try It Out

Make a "Book of Records" for your class. You can include information like this: the oldest student in your class, the student who can jump the farthest, the student who has the most cousins. Be sure to include photos or drawings in your book.

The Oldest Person

The oldest person lived to be more than 120 years old. She was Jeanne Calment of France. She was born in 1875 and was still living in the 1990s.

The Fastest Runners

In 1994, Leroy Burrell ran the fastest 100-meter race. He ran the race in 9.85 seconds. This is about 23 miles (37 kilometers) per hour. Florence Griffith Joyner has run the fastest in the women's 100-meter race. Her time was 10.49 seconds.

The Most Push-ups

Charles Servizio of the United States did 46,001 push-ups in one day.

The Longest Gum Wrapper Chain

Gary Duschl of Canada made the longest chain from gum wrappers. It was 12,105 feet (3,690 meters) long.

? Think About It

What other information do you think would be interesting to include in a Book of Records?

Would you want your name in a Book of Records? What could you do to get into a record book?

Turn! Turn! Turn!

by Pete Seeger

To everything, turn, turn, turn,
There is a season, turn, turn, turn,
And a time for every purpose under heaven.

A time to be born, a time to die;
A time to plant, a time to reap;
A time to kill, a time to heal;
A time to laugh, a time to weep.

A time to build up, a time to break down;
A time to dance, a time to mourn;
A time to cast away stones;
A time to gather stones together.

? Think About It

The song has many words that are opposites. Can
you find them? Does looking for opposites help you
understand the meaning of words?

Why do you think the song uses opposites? What is
the song saying about the changes in life?

Tell what you learned.

1. What is a "growth spurt"? How does it make teenagers feel awkward?

2. What is heredity? What are some traits that are determined by heredity?

3. Explain why using your foot to measure length is, or is not, as good as using a ruler.

4. Make the chart with the food groups. Write the names of foods from each group that you ate yesterday.

Food Group	Examples
Grains	
Vegetables	
Fruit	
Dairy products	
Meat, poultry, dry beans, fish, eggs, nuts	
Fats, oils, sweets	

5. Which of the facts from *The Guinness Book of Records* did you find most interesting?

6. If you could set a record, what would it be?

Life Cycles of Plants

Word Bank

- **flower**
- **fruit**
- **leaf**
- **roots**
- **stem**
- **trunk**

Tell what you know.

These plants grow in different regions of the world. Can you name any of the plants? Can you identify their parts?

Talk About It

What plants grow where you live? Which plants grow in other places where you have lived?

Parts of a Flower

Plants are important. They make food for themselves. They make food for animals and people.

Most plants have flowers. These include tall trees and the vegetables that grow in gardens.

Flowers have four main parts. Each part has a different function.

The **sepals** cover and protect the flower buds until the flowers open.

sepal

Petals protect the parts of the flowers that make seeds. They are often very colorful.

Stamens make pollen. Pollen grains are the male cells of the flower. The stamens are inside the petals.

The **pistil** makes and holds the egg cells. Egg cells are the female cells of the flower. A seed develops when an egg cell and pollen combine.

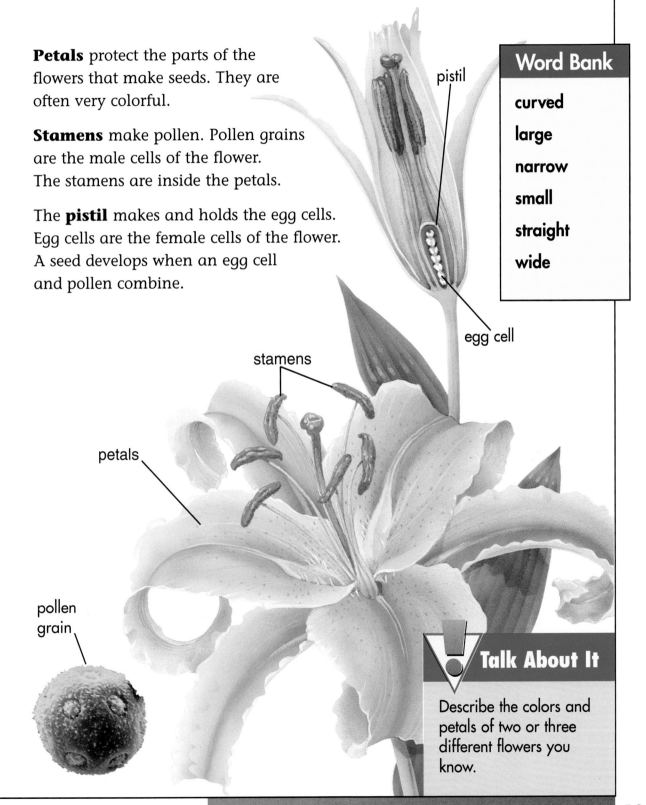

pistil

egg cell

stamens

petals

pollen grain

Talk About It

Describe the colors and petals of two or three different flowers you know.

Life Cycle of a Flowering Plant

Flowers are important in the life cycle of most plants. Flowers help the plants reproduce.

Pollen grains combine with the eggs in a flower to produce seeds. This process is called **pollination.** The flower that is pollinated can be on the same plant or on a different plant.

Bees and other insects help some plants pollinate. They carry pollen from the stamens of flowers to the pistils. Wind helps other plants pollinate. Wind carries the pollen through the air. The pollen moves from the stamen of one plant to the pistil of another plant.

After pollination, the flower dries up and falls off. Now the plant produces seeds. These seeds might fall to the ground. Wind or animals might carry them to another place. The seeds then grow into new plants. These new plants then produce flowers. And the life cycle of the plant repeats.

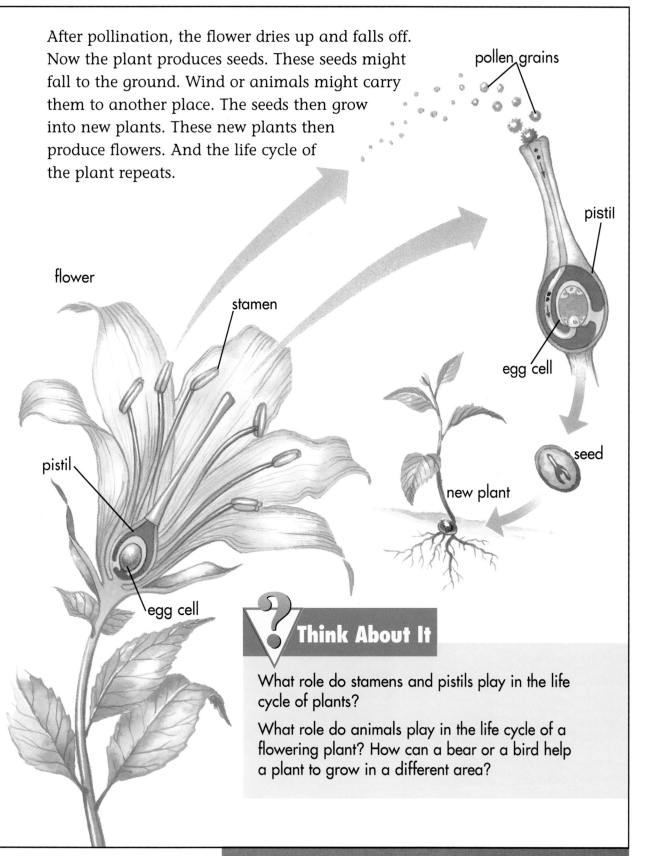

pollen grains

pistil

egg cell

seed

new plant

flower

stamen

pistil

egg cell

? Think About It

What role do stamens and pistils play in the life cycle of plants?

What role do animals play in the life cycle of a flowering plant? How can a bear or a bird help a plant to grow in a different area?

Eating Plants

What parts of plants do you eat? You eat the seeds of plants when you eat corn, rice, or peanuts. You eat the stems of plants when you eat asparagus. You eat the leaves of plants when you eat lettuce or spinach. You eat the flowers of plants when you eat cauliflower or broccoli. You eat the roots of plants when you eat radishes or carrots.

You eat the fruit of plants when you eat apples, tomatoes, and peaches. The fruit is the part of a plant that contains seeds. Some fruits, such as avocados, contain only one seed. Other fruits, such as raspberries, contain many seeds.

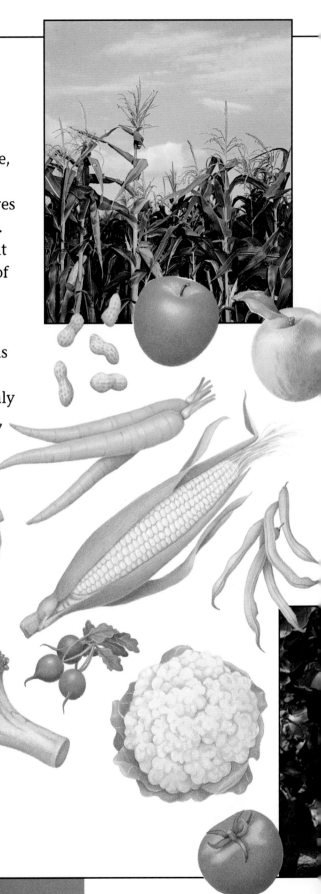

Try It Out

Find an advertisement from a supermarket. Look back at the Food Pyramid on page 8. Make a list of foods that are plants or that are from plants. What food group does each belong to? What part of the plant do we eat?

Make a chart. Write the names of the plants you eat for a week. Write each name under the correct column. Do you eat the seeds, stems, leaves, flowers, roots, or fruit of the plant?

The Plant Parts I Eat Every Day						
	Seeds	Stems	Leaves	Flowers	Roots	Fruits
Monday						
Tuesday						
Wednesday						
Thursday						
Friday						
Saturday						
Sunday						

Write About It

What parts of plants do you eat the most often? What parts of the plants do you like the best?

Numbers in Plants

In 1225, an Italian mathematician named Leonardo Fibonacci developed a series of numbers. The series is called the Fibonacci sequence. The series of numbers starts with two 1s. Each number following is the sum of the two numbers before it.

Here is the start of the Fibonacci sequence. Can you fill in the missing numbers?

1	
1	(0 + 1)
2	(1 + 1)
3	(2 + 1)
5	(3 + 2)
8	(5 + 3)
?	(8 + 5)
?	(? + 8)

What do these numbers have to do with plants?

The leaves of some plants grow in Fibonacci sequences. Find a plant in which the leaves grow out of the stem. Find two leaves directly above one another. Count the leaves. Count the bottom leaf as zero. Stop counting at the top leaf. The number is a Fibonacci number.

The seeds on a sunflower grow in two sets of spirals. There are usually 21 spirals that grow in one direction, and 34 that grow in the other direction. These are Fibonacci numbers.

When you count parts on many other plants, the numbers are in the Fibonacci sequence.

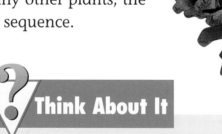

Think About It

What is wrong in the following Fibonacci sequences?

1, 1, 2, 3, 5, 13, 34, 55

1, 1, 2, 3, 5, 8, 13, 34, 55, 89, 144, 375, 610

Continue these sequences.

1, 3, 4, 7, 11, 18, 29, ___

1, 3, 6, 10, 15, 21, 28, 36, ____

1, 3, 7, 15, 31, 63, 127, ___

The Story of Johnny Appleseed

by Meridel Le Sueur

Reader's Tip
Jonathan Chapman was born in 1774 in Massachusetts (in the eastern part of the United States). Jonathan Chapman decided to travel and plant apple trees in the West. Over the years, people told many stories about this folk hero called "Johnny Appleseed."

It was lonely making America. It was a big, big country. It was a deep, wide country. And there were no apple trees, no big round apples, no little bright, tart apples. No apples at all!

It would have been very sad, but there was a man who thought it would be very lonely making America without any apple trees blooming early in the spring, without red apples hanging on the trees in Ohio, Illinois, and Iowa, in the frosty fall. This man's name was Jonathan Chapman.

My grandmother in Ohio saw him going by her house in the spring, in the fall. The geese flying in a wedge in the sky looked down and saw him traveling along, wearing his gunnysack coat, his books stuffed in the front of it, and on his head his stewpot hat to keep him cool in the heat of the day. When night came, he cooked his mush in it. He never wore any shoes if he could help it.

Strategy Tip
Use Pictures for Meaning
The story tells about the kind of clothes that Johnny wore. You can use the picture on the page to help you understand the words.

Strategy Tip
Locate Places
Find the states named
in the story on a map.
People from the East
were beginning to move
west in large numbers
during the 1800s.
Locating places should
help you understand
the story better.

Jonathan Chapman was a lean and lonesome
man who loved apples. He was a man who never
threw an apple core away in his life. When he was a
young man, he was walking in Pennsylvania.
Beyond was the wilderness.

Jonathan stopped to get something to eat and he
heard a child crying from a covered wagon which
was going on into the wilderness.

The child was crying to his mother, "I don't want to go. I want to stay here."

The child's mother was angry. She said, "You can't stay here. Your father is going west. And you must go west too."

The child cried, "I don't want to leave the apple trees."

Reader's Tip

When settlers moved out west, they put everything they owned into a wagon. They covered the top of the wagon with canvas to hold everything in and protect it. They used horses or oxen to pull these covered wagons.

Strategy Tip
Understand Character
What do you learn about
Johnny when he tells the
child not to cry?

Jonathan said to the crying child, "I love apple trees too. They are my children. I love apples because they have such kind hearts. The trees are so generous. A tree has not one blossom but thousands. If God made no other fruit but the apple, His work would have been well done. Don't cry, child. I will plant thousands of tiny seeds in the wilderness where you are going, in Illinois, in Indiana, in Kentucky, and the apple trees will spring up and bloom in the spring."

So the child stopped crying and smiled at Jonathan and waved from the back of the covered wagon as they went into the wilderness, into the land of the Indian and the snake, of the buffalo and the deep grass.

The land that had no apple trees.

Jonathan was standing by a cider mill. He saw big piles of apple mash and in the mash were all the tiny brown apple seeds. He had a bright idea.

Jonathan got a sack and sat down and began to pick each seed out of the apple mash and put it into the sack.

A man came along and said, "What are you doing?"

Jonathan said, "I am going to fill this sack with apple seeds."

The man said, "And what are you going to do with a sack of apple seeds?"

"I am going to follow the covered wagons out of town toward the sun," Jonathan said. "I am going to plant them. The soil must be good there and the children are crying for apples."

And the man laughed. "What an idea, carrying seed like a bird!"

Others had gathered by this time, and they were all laughing at Jonathan squatting in the mash, putting apple seeds into a sack.

"Ho!" they laughed. "Look! What's your name?"

"Johnny," he answered them.

"Ho!" the men laughed. "Johnny Appleseed!"

So that was what he was called after that, my grandmother told me—Johnny Appleseed.

The children ran out, when he came into the village clearings in the wilderness, shouting, "Here comes Johnny Appleseed."

The deer came with him to the edge of the forest and said, "Good-bye, Johnny Appleseed."

The little round eyes of the robin, the wren, the marsh birds and the swans saw him walking with his pack of apple seeds on his back and they knew Johnny Appleseed was going by.

Strategy Tip
Series
A series is a list of words joined by the word and. Often the words in a series are related. All the words in this series are names of birds.

Language Tip
Vocabulary
People use a shovel to dig, an ax to cut trees, and a hoe to prepare the ground for planting seeds.

Study Tip
Understand Character
In many stories, characters' actions tell you about the kinds of person they are. Other peoples' reactions to a character also give clues to a character's personality.

He followed the sun every day, lying down in the fields at night; rising, walking west with the sun. And on his back he carried a gunnysack, and in the sack thousands of apple seeds went with him, which would be great trees along the valley by the time you were born.

And all the animals knew, all the birds and the buffalo and the deer and the bear knew that he carried a shovel, an axe, and a hoe, but never a gun.

My grandmother, too, told me that he never carried a gun. My grandmother said that he was the friend of all the beasts and birds of America.

It was early spring in Licking Creek, Ohio, my grandmother said, when she first saw Johnny Appleseed coming through the forest with his pack of apple seeds in a sack over his shoulder.

He was tall, she said, skinny, with long black hair falling to his bony shoulders. But it was the eyes, she said, you couldn't forget.

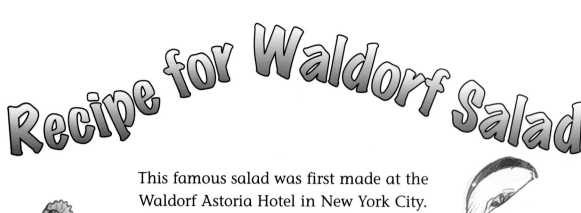

Recipe for Waldorf Salad

This famous salad was first made at the
Waldorf Astoria Hotel in New York City.
It is very tasty, and it is made with apples!

Serves 6

1 pound of apples (red and green)
2 tablespoons lemon juice
3 stalks celery, chopped
1/2 cup walnuts, chopped
1/2 cup mayonnaise
Salt and pepper

Wash and cut the apples. Slice them into a bowl.
Add the celery, walnuts, lemon juice, and
mayonnaise. Season with salt and pepper.
Then mix. Keep the salad in the refrigerator
until you are ready to serve it.
(Mayonnaise can spoil easily if it is not kept cold.)

 Talk About It

Which food groups are
in a Waldorf Salad? Is it
a healthful choice for a
snack? Why or why not?

Tell what you learned.

1. Draw a flower. Label the four main parts. Tell what each part of the flower does.

2. Describe the life cycle of a flowering plant.

3. Do you think Johnny Appleseed was a hero? Why or why not?

4. What is the most interesting fact you learned about plants? What else would you like to learn about plants?

Weather

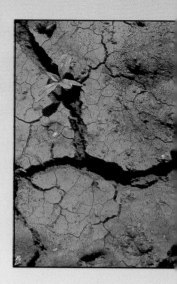

Tell what you know.

What kind of weather do you like? Why?

What kinds of problems can weather cause?

Talk About It

What is the weather like today?

What is the weather usually like on your birthday?

What kind of weather is "bad"?

What kind of weather is "good"?

CHAPTER 3

Changing Weather

What makes the weather change?

Air is all around the earth. The air is hot in some places on the earth and cold in other places. What makes air hot or cold? What makes the weather change? Large bodies of air called **air masses** control changes in the temperature and the weather.

The air above the earth's surface is not the same everywhere. The air above a cold place gets cold and forms a cold air mass. The air above a hot place gets hot and forms a hot air mass. So the air above snow and ice is cold. Is the air above a desert hot or cold?

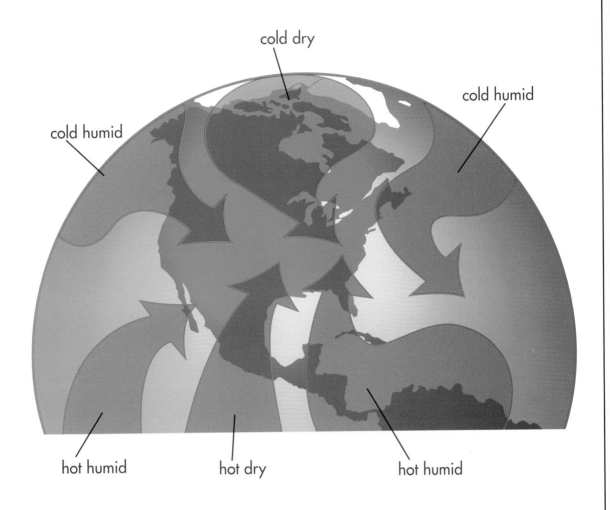

cold dry

cold humid

cold humid

hot humid

hot dry

hot humid

The air in an air mass can be hot or cold. The air
in an air mass can also be dry or humid (wet).
An air mass that forms above land has mostly
dry air. An air mass that forms above water has
mostly humid air.

Talk About It

An air mass is forming over your school. Is it hot or
cold? Is it dry or humid? Why do you think so?

Does air have weight?

Do this experiment to find out if air has weight.

Things You Need

string—about 12 to 18 inches (30 to 46 centimeters) long

ruler—12 inches (about 30 centimeters) long

two balloons—exactly the same size

tape (clear)

Follow these steps.

1. Tie the string to the exact middle of the ruler.

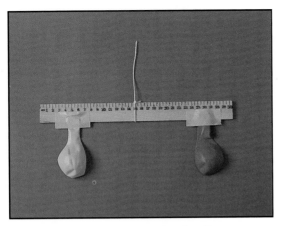

2. Do not blow up the balloons. Tape each balloon exactly 2 inches (5 centimeters) from each end of the ruler.

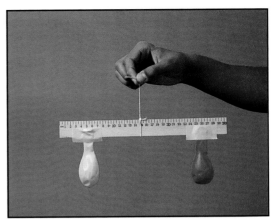

3. Pick up the loose end of the string. Hold the end of the string up in the air so that the ruler is not touching the table. What happens?

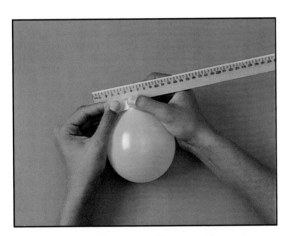

4. Remove one balloon. Blow it up. Tie it tightly. Tape the balloon with air in it back onto the ruler at the place where it was before. If you picked up the string now, which side of the ruler will go down? Why do you think so?

5. Now pick up the ruler by the string. What happens to the ruler? Which balloon is heavier?

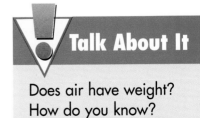

Talk About It

Does air have weight? How do you know?

Air Pressure and Storms

Do you feel air pushing all around you? Air pushes down on the earth and on you all the time. This push is called **air pressure**.

Warm air and cold air have different weights. Warm air is lighter than cold air. Warm air rises. So warm air doesn't push down very hard on the earth. An area with a warm air mass over it is called a **low pressure area**.

Cold air pushes down very hard on the earth. So an area with a cold air mass over it is called a **high pressure area**.

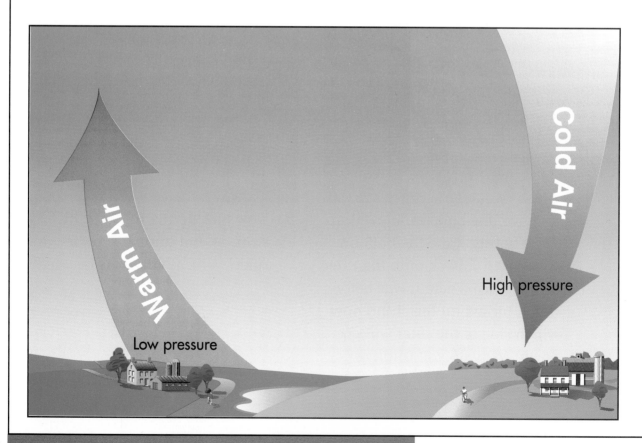

Warm Air

Cold Air

Low pressure

High pressure

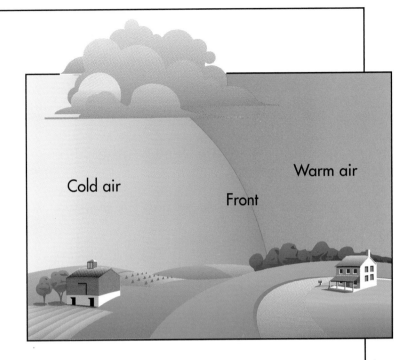

Cold air

Warm air

Front

The place where two different air masses meet is called a **front.** The front forms a boundary between the two air masses.

Storms often happen at fronts. A cold air mass pushes into a warm air mass. It makes the warm air rise very fast. The moving air causes wind. As the warm air rises, it cools. Water in the air forms clouds. Then the water falls to the earth as rain or snow.

A cold air mass pushing into a warm air mass can cause a thunderstorm. A thunderstorm has wind, rain, thunder, and lightning!

Write About It

What causes a storm? Draw a diagram and explain.

Weather Idioms and Sayings

English has many idioms with weather words. In the idioms, the weather words take on special meanings. Here are some weather idioms to describe people.

A person who gets angry easily is **stormy.**

A person who is a bit sick is **under the weather.**

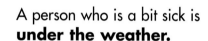

A person who is always daydreaming has his or her **head in the clouds.**

A person who can run fast can **run like the wind.**

People also can use weather words to talk about life in general.

When it rains hard, people say it is **raining cats and dogs.**

People know that bad things may also have something good related to them. People say, **April showers bring May flowers.**

People also try to be ready for a bad time. Sometimes people save money for this reason. People say, **save for a rainy day.**

? Think About It

What do you think this weather saying means? "Everybody talks about the weather, but nobody does anything about it."

Do you know any sayings about the weather in your native language? What are they? What do they mean in English?

Why the Monsoon Comes Each Year

Retold by Dorothy Lewis Robertson

Language Tip
Vocabulary
A *monsoon* is a seasonal wind that brings heavy rains to South Asia every year. This folk tale is from Vietnam, a country in Southeast Asia.

The Princess Mi Nuong was sad. She sat quietly with downcast eyes while a handmaiden combed her glossy, black hair and idly smoothed a fold in the silk of her gown. When the last jade pin was fastened in her hair and the handmaiden held up a mirror, she pushed it away without even glancing in it. She already knew what the mirror would show her: a tiny new wrinkle between her eyes. It was this new wrinkle that made her sad. She was growing old and she was husbandless.

It wasn't that she was ugly or lame or bad tempered.
She had had many suitors. Some were handsome and many
had come from foreign lands, but not one had gained the
consent of her father, the Emperor. Like many fathers with
only one child, he believed that no one was good enough
for his charming daughter. For her he wanted someone rich
and distinguished and, above all, powerful. Years had
passed since the last suitor had proposed and been
declined, and it looked as though the Princess would
remain single forever.

Strategy Tip
Recognize Main
Characters
When you read a story,
ask yourself, "Who is
important in this
story?"

Language Tip
Vocabulary
Betrothal means
engagement to be
married.

Then one day two strangers appeared at the Emperor's court. Both were very handsome, both were very rich, and one was the powerful Spirit of the Sea and the other was the equally powerful Spirit of the Mountain. Since both suitors arrived at exactly the same time, and met with equal favor in the eyes of the Emperor, he was hard put to choose between them. So he told them that whoever first brought his betrothal gifts the next day would have the hand of the Princess and could leave with her immediately.

The Spirit of the Sea rushed back to the ocean and summoned his men. He commanded them to search for the most perfect pearls, the tastiest crabs, and the juiciest squid. The Spirit of the Mountain climbed to the highest peak and gathered his men about him. Then he opened his magic book and wished for the gifts he wanted to present to the Princess. He wished for his men to find a chest of diamonds and emeralds that had been hidden in a dark cave in the mountains for hundreds of years, and he wished for them to fill baskets with rare fruits that couldn't be grown at the Emperor's court.

Strategy Tip
Understand Detail
In this story, both the Spirit of the Sea and the Spirit of the Mountain want to marry Mi Nuong. Each needs to show how strong he is. What does each spirit do to meet the challenge?

Presently the men appeared before the Spirit of the Mountain with the casket of jewels and baskets of strawberries, peaches, and grapes. Then, while the Spirit of the Sea was still searching the depths of the ocean for his gifts, the Spirit of the Mountain with his men was on his way down the mountainside to be first at the gates of the Emperor's palace. He arrived there just as dawn was breaking, and claimed Mi Nuong as his bride. The Emperor was delighted with the gifts of jewels and fruit, and felt that surely he had made a good match for his daughter. He sent her off with the Spirit of the Mountain and promised to visit her in her new home as soon as she was settled.

Mi Nuong and her husband were barely outside the gates of the Emperor's palace when along the road from the sea came the Spirit of the Sea with his men bearing great trays of pearls and dishes of delicious sea food. When the Spirit of the Sea saw that he was late by just a few minutes and that the sun was barely over the horizon, he was very angry. He suspected that the Spirit of the Mountain had used some tricks to get there first and so he commanded his followers to pursue the Spirit of the Mountain and take Mi Nuong away from him.

Language Tip
Vocabulary
Bearing means carrying.

Strategy Tip
Understand Plot
In a competition, one person wins and the other is defeated. The Spirit of the Mountain won, and got Mi Nuong as his bride. What did the defeated Spirit of the Sea do then?

With that, the wind began to blow and the rain fell and the ocean rose higher and higher. Soon foaming waves were breaking over the land, and the people had to flee for their lives. All of the creatures of the sea turned into soldiers of the Spirit of the Sea and ran screaming up the road to overtake the Spirit of the Mountain before he could get to the high ground where he ruled. Wherever they passed, the rivers rose into floods, houses were washed away, and whole cities were left in ruins. The water rose higher and higher, until waves were breaking at the foot of the mountain, but still the Spirit of the Sea had not caught up with Mi Nuong. Now the Spirit of the Mountain ordered his men to throw huge logs and boulders down on the Spirit of the Sea and his forces.

The battle between the two most powerful spirits continued both day and night, and the poor people of the villages prayed for them to stop. Many had been drowned in the flood; some had been struck by lightning. Their crops had been washed away, as well as their homes. Finally, the Spirit of the Mountain used his magic wishing book to wish his mountain to grow higher. Then he took Mi Nuong and his men to the very highest peak, well out of reach of the Spirit of the Sea.

When the Spirit of the Sea saw that his attempt to overcome the Spirit of the Mountain was in vain, he retreated with his soldiers back to the ocean, taking the flood waters with him. But so angry was he at his defeat that every year he tries again to defeat the Spirit of the Mountain and win the Princess Mi Nuong to be his own wife. Every year he sends storms and floods up the river valleys to the very foot of the mountain where Mi Nuong still lives with her husband. And each year he is again defeated and forced to withdraw to his home in the ocean. And that is why the monsoon comes each year in Viet Nam.

Study Tips
Characters' Problems
In life, people have problems. In stories, characters have problems, too. At the beginning of the story, what problem does the princess have? What problems do the two suitors have? At the end of the story, what problem does the Spirit of the Sea have?

Strategy Tip
Understand the Big Idea
Folk stories are often used to explain why something happens in nature. What does this folk tale explain?

Lotsa Winds

by Sonja Dunn
with Lou Pamenter

How many sounds
do the four winds make?

Hundreds and hundreds
for goodness' sake

Listen listen
to the sound
As they whoosh
around and 'round

Missssssssssssstral
SSSSSSSSSSSSSSSirroco
ChChChChChChChChChChinooooooook
Monssoooooooooooooooooooooon
Doldruuuuuuuuuuuuuuuuum
Traaaaaaaaaaade wiiiiiiiind
Northsouthwesteast wiiiiiiiinds
ZZZZZZZZZZZZZZZZZZZephyr

If you make those sounds again
You may start a HURRICANE!

? Think About It

This poem contains the names of many types of
winds. These names come from different parts of the
world. What do all these different names say about
the importance of wind in many different cultures?

Why does the poem's author repeat some letters in
the names?

Tell what you learned.

1. Explain how you learned that air has weight. Draw pictures of your experiment.

2. What challenge did the Emperor give to the two suitors for Princess Mi Nuong? How did they meet that challenge?

3. Make a list of the way weather challenges people in your town. How do people try to meet that challenge?

4. How do changes in the weather affect you?

Predicting the Weather

Word Bank

newspaper

observation

radio

television

weather forecast

Tell what you know.

How do you find out what the weather will be?

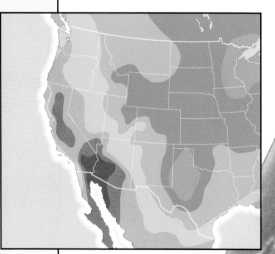

Rain, Rain and More Rain

by Bob Dyselick

Why is it important to
know what the weather
will be?

Where can you get daily
weather information?

The Work of Meteorologists

A **meteorologist** is a scientist who studies the weather. A meteorologist studies the weather to help people plan their activities. A meteorologist can help people plan for the next day or for the next season. People want to know what kind of clothes to wear tomorrow or if they should prepare for an especially cold winter.

A meteorologist can help people plan what to ▶ wear by predicting if it will snow tomorrow.

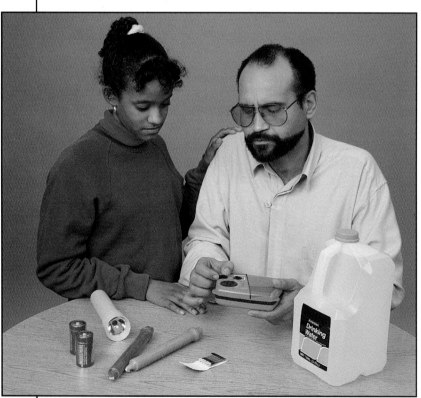

▲ A meteorologist can tell people when to get ready for a bad storm.

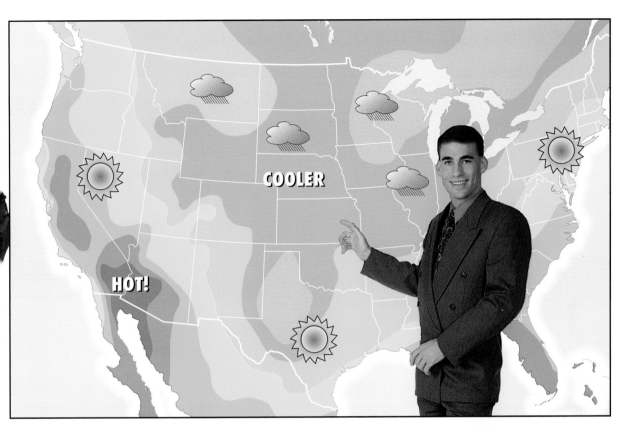

▲ A meteorologist can tell people what kind of weather their friends and relatives are having in faraway places.

People who want to be meteorologists take courses in math, statistics, computer science, chemistry, and physics in college. As meteorologists, they study information on air pressure, temperature, wind speed, and other factors. They use computer models of the world's weather to say what they think will happen.

In 1994, there were about 6,600 meteorologists in the United States. About half of them worked for the government. Others worked for TV or radio stations, universities, and private companies.

Talk About It

Would you like to be a meteorologist? Why or why not?

What tools do meteorologists use?

Meteorologists use many tools to help them collect information about the weather. The tools help meteorologists measure things. Meteorologists keep records of the weather, too. The records help meteorologists understand weather patterns.

Meteorologists use a **thermometer** to measure ▶ temperature.

Meteorologists use a **barometer** to measure air ▶ pressure. A change in air pressure means that the weather is going to change. When the level of the barometer falls, it means that the air pressure is changing. A storm is coming!

Meteorologists use an **anemometer** to ▶ measure wind speed. An anemometer spins in the wind and records how fast the wind is blowing.

Meteorologists use a **rain gauge** to measure ▶ how much rain has fallen. Rain is one form of **precipitation,** or water. Other forms are snow, hail, and dew.

Meteorologists use **radar** to watch a storm that is far away. Meteorologists use this information to help them predict what direction a storm is going and how fast it is moving.

▲ Meteorologists use sky **satellites** to find out about the weather over very large areas. Satellites can send back information and photographs to the meteorologists on the ground. Meteorologists use this information and the photographs to learn more about storms and other kinds of weather all over the earth.

Think About It

Meteorologists use many tools to predict the weather, but their predictions are not always correct. Why not?

Who uses weather forecasts?

Many TV news programs tell about the weather. Radio stations tell about the weather, too. Newspapers print weather **forecasts** and weather maps.

Why is there so much talk and writing about the weather? People want to know about the weather so they can make plans. People need to know about the weather so they can prepare for dangerous situations.

Airport managers need to know about the weather to keep people and airplanes safe. A weather forecast will let airport managers know when to have snowplows ready.

Airline companies need to know about high winds and storms that might be dangerous for their airplanes in the sky.

Farmers need to know about the weather so they can plan their work. A weather forecast can tell farmers when they need to do special things to protect their crops. For example, a forecast may say that there will be low temperatures that will damage unprotected crops.

Builders need to know about the weather so they can know when it will be too cold to do some kinds of construction work.

School principals need to know about the weather so they can cancel school if it will be too cold, snowy, or icy for students and teachers to get to school safely.

Talk About It

Do you use weather forecasts? How do weather forecasts help you?

Talk with some people where you live. Find out how they use weather forecasts.

You can measure wind speed.

Airline pilots and other people need to know how fast the wind is blowing. You can measure the speed of the wind by doing this experiment. Work with a partner.

Things You Need

strong thread or fine nylon fishing line –about 12 inches (30 centimeters) long

tape a ping-pong ball a protractor–the biggest one you can find

Follow these steps.

1. Tape one end of the string to the ping-pong ball. Tape the other end to the exact center point on the base of the protractor. Now you have made an anemometer.

2. Test your anemometer. Hold it level and away from your body. The flat side of the protractor should be up. Make sure the ball can swing freely.

3. Test your anemometer. There is no wind in your classroom, so the ball should hang straight down. The string will hang at the 90 degree mark on the protractor.

4. Now go outside on a windy day. Hold your anemometer so the narrow side points into the wind. Hold the anemometer away from your body. The ping-pong ball will swing. Ask your partner to read and record the angle on the protractor.

5. Use the chart that follows to determine how fast the wind was blowing when you measured it.

How fast is the wind blowing?														
Angle														
90	85	80	75	70	65	60	55	50	45	40	35	30	25	20
Miles Per Hour														
0	5.8	8.2	10.1	11.8	13.4	14.9	16.4	18.0	19.6	21.4	23.4	25.8	28.7	32.5
Kilometers Per Hour														
0	9.3	13.2	16.3	19.0	21.6	24.0	26.4	29.0	31.5	34.4	37.6	41.5	46.2	52.3

My Record

Date	Wind Speed

 Try It Out

Try this experiment on several days that are windy and cloudy. Take pictures of the sky. Point the lens of the camera up towards the clouds. Take several pictures about two minutes apart of the same area of sky. When you look at the finished pictures, you will be able to see the movement of the clouds.

Reading Weather Maps

A weather map like the one on this page shows what weather is forecasted for the United States. The map uses colors, numbers, and letters. The map key tells what these colors, numbers, and letters mean.

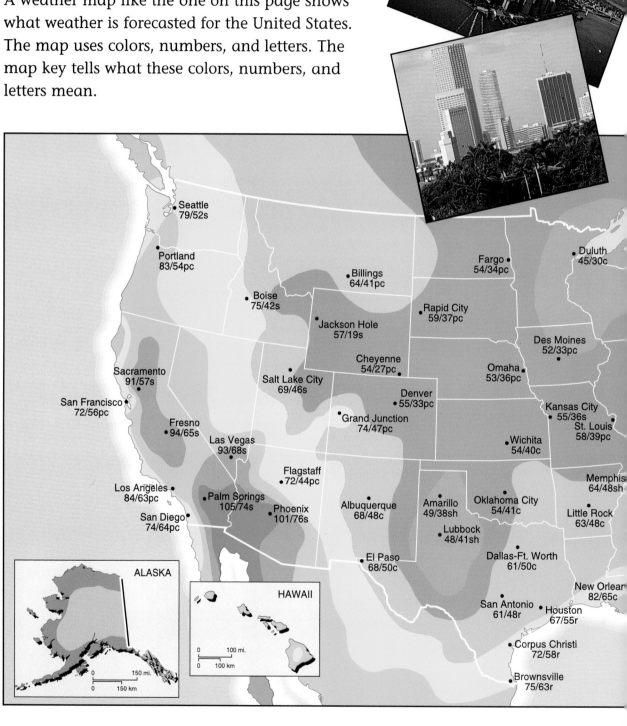

Seattle
79/52s

Portland
83/54pc

Billings
64/41pc

Fargo
54/34pc

Duluth
45/30c

Boise
75/42s

Jackson Hole
57/19s

Rapid City
59/37pc

Des Moines
52/33pc

Sacramento
91/57s

Salt Lake City
69/46s

Cheyenne
54/27pc

Omaha
53/36pc

San Francisco
72/56pc

Denver
55/33pc

Grand Junction
74/47pc

Kansas City
55/36s

St. Louis
58/39pc

Fresno
94/65s

Las Vegas
93/68s

Wichita
54/40c

Flagstaff
72/44pc

Memphis
64/48sh

Los Angeles
84/63pc

Palm Springs
105/74s

Phoenix
101/76s

Albuquerque
68/48c

Amarillo
49/38sh

Oklahoma City
54/41c

Little Rock
63/48c

San Diego
74/64pc

Lubbock
48/41sh

Dallas-Ft. Worth
61/50c

El Paso
68/50c

New Orleans
82/65c

ALASKA

HAWAII

San Antonio
61/48r

Houston
67/55r

0   100 mi.
0   100 km

Corpus Christi
72/58r

0   150 mi.
0   150 km

Brownsville
75/63r

United States Weather Map

Numbers (in degrees Fahrenheit):
today's forecast high, tomorrow morning's forecast low.

Below 10	10s	20s	30s	40s	50s	60s	70s	80s	90s	100s

c	Cloudy	sh	Showers
pc	Partly cloudy	sn	Snow
r	Rain	sf	Snow flurries
s	Sun	t	Thunderstorms

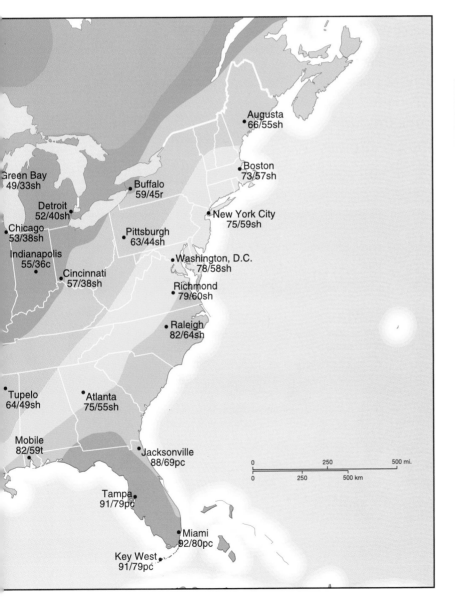

Augusta
66/55sh

Boston
73/57sh

Green Bay
49/33sh

Buffalo
59/45r

New York City
75/59sh

Detroit
52/40sh

Chicago
53/38sh

Pittsburgh
63/44sh

Indianapolis
55/36c

Washington, D.C.
78/58sh

Cincinnati
57/38sh

Richmond
79/60sh

Raleigh
82/64sh

Tupelo
64/49sh

Atlanta
75/55sh

Mobile
82/59t

Jacksonville
88/69pc

Tampa
91/79pc

Miami
92/80pc

Key West
91/79pc

0   250   500 mi.

0   250   500 km

Try It Out

Work with a partner. Use the map to answer these questions. Then make up your own. Ask your partner the questions you make up.

What two states are predicted to have the highest temperatures?

What temperature range does the color yellow stand for?

What is the high temperature predicted to be in Brownsville, Texas?

Is it predicted to be cooler in New York City or in Miami, Florida?

What is the weather predicted to be like where you live?

A Stormy Weather Forecast

Nancy: It's noon—time for the WBAM Radio Midday Weather Report. So now let's go directly to meteorologist Keith Baker at the WBAM weather center.

Keith: Good afternoon, Nancy. . . . I'm afraid that the heavy rain storms of last night are going to continue. The severe weather front is going to be stalled in our area until at least midnight tonight. So far, we have officially recorded more than 9 inches of rain since yesterday at 7 P.M. As most of you know, this large amount of precipitation has caused flooding in many city neighborhoods.

Word Bank

breezy

calm

clear

cloudy

overcast

precipitation

temperature

wind speed

Within the last hour, the wind has increased in speed. We are recording gusts of up to 40 miles per hour on the WBAM anemometer right now. Because of these high winds, the state police have closed our freeways to all truck and bus traffic for the rest of the day.

At noon, the official temperature at City Hall was 48 degrees. That temperature, along with the heavy precipitation and high winds, will give us a pretty lousy afternoon and evening. So stay indoors if possible folks!

Nancy: Thanks, Keith, for bringing us up to date on this continuing situation. . . . And now to the national news. . . .

Write About It

Work with a partner to write and perform your own radio station weather forecast. Talk about the temperature, wind, clouds, and precipitation for today and tonight.

Weather

Anonymous

Whether the weather be fine,
Or whether the weather be not,
Whether the weather be cold,
Or whether the weather be hot,
We'll weather the weather
Whatever the weather
Whether we like it or not.

? Think About It

What idea about
weather does this poem
suggest? Do you think
that the idea is right?

Raindrop

by John Travers Moore

A drop
of water
    hit my window,
Felt the pull
to downward places—
Joined another drop—
another,
    Still one more
        and more
          until
    it
      zigzagged
   rapidly
    into a stream
      of crystal
       and ran
       to the
       bottom
       of
       the
       pane.

Talk About It

Concrete poetry uses shape to suggest meaning. Why is this a good example of a concrete poem?

Good Day Sunshine

by Paul McCartney

Good day sunshine, good day sunshine,
good day sunshine.
I need to laugh, and when the sun is out,
I've got something I can laugh about.
I feel good in a special way,
I'm in love, and it's a sunny day.
Good day sunshine, good day sunshine,
good day sunshine.
We take a walk, the sun is shining down,
burns my feet as they touch the ground.
Good day sunshine, good day sunshine,
good day sunshine.

Tell what you learned.

1. Why do people listen to weather forecasts? How do you use weather forecasts?

2. Make a weather dictionary for the students who will study weather next year. Put in all the words you think are important, and draw pictures to help explain them.

3. What other information would you like to learn about weather forecasting?

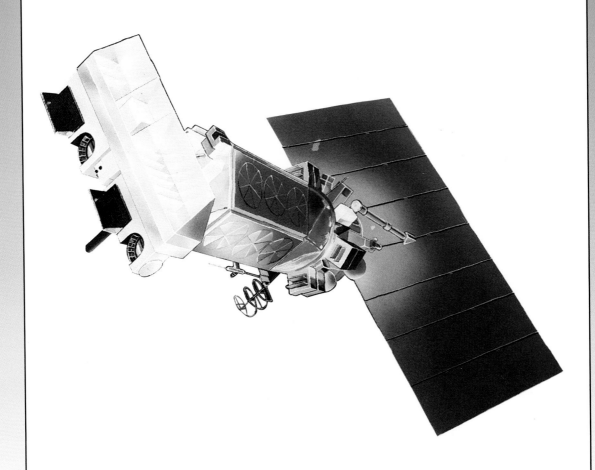

The Civil War

Tell what you know.

What is war?
These pictures are from the 1860s, during the
U.S. Civil War. What things do the pictures
tell about the war?

What wars do you know about? What countries did the fighting? Why did they fight?

The United States Before the Civil War

A Nation Divided

In 1861, the states in the United States were divided into two kinds. In the North, slavery was mostly **illegal,** or against the law. In the South slavery was **legal.** It was not against the law.

The states were different in other ways, too. In the northern states, people had left farms to work in factories. They made many kinds of products. There were many roads, canals, and railroads. These made it possible to move people and goods quickly and cheaply.

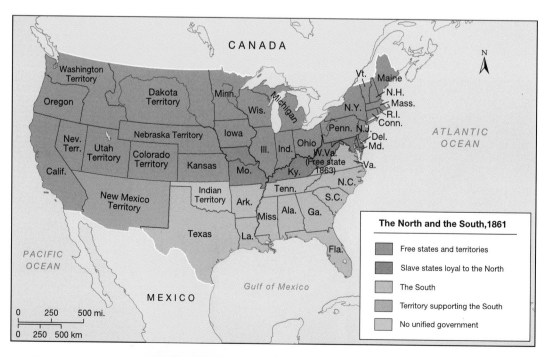

The North and the South, 1861	
	Free states and territories
	Slave states loyal to the North
	The South
	Territory supporting the South
	No unified government

In the southern states, most people still lived on farms. There were few railroads, canals, roads, or factories.

These differences caused problems between the North and the South. Each side was afraid of the other getting too much power. Every time a new state became part of the nation, people asked the same questions: Would slavery be legal or illegal in the new state? Who had the right to decide—the state government or the federal government in Washington?

Talk About It

Talk about where you were born. Were most people there farmers or factory workers or some of both?

Slavery

By the 1800s, growing cotton was an important business in the South. Farmers grew cotton on farms and large **plantations.** Farmers needed more and more workers for their cotton fields.

When the Civil War began in 1861, about 3.9 million African American slaves lived in the United States. Almost all of them lived in the South and worked on the farms and plantations of white families.

Slaves had no **rights.** They could be bought and sold like animals. They were not allowed to learn to read and write. They worked for long hours and received no pay. They were fed very little. They were beaten if they did not obey orders. Sometimes, slaves tried to escape. They were often caught and returned. Then they were punished.

Word Bank

farm

harvest

pick

plant

Think About It

What kind of work did most slaves do?

Imagine that you were captured, taken to a faraway country, and sold. What would you do?

Those Who Opposed Slavery

By the mid-1800s, many people in the United States opposed slavery. These people were called **abolitionists.** They wanted to abolish, or end, all slavery. William Lloyd Garrison was an abolitionist. He started a newspaper called *The Liberator.* It opposed slavery.

Frederick Douglass was another abolitionist. Douglass was an escaped slave. He made abolitionist speeches and started an abolitionist newspaper called *The North Star.* He became a major leader of the abolitionist cause.

William Lloyd Garrison

Frederick Douglass

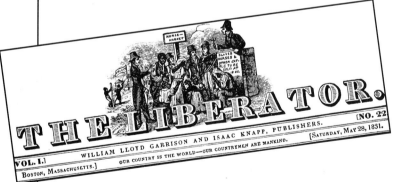

In 1852, northerner Harriet Beecher Stowe wrote a novel opposing slavery. It was called *Uncle Tom's Cabin*. Stowe's book sold more than 300,000 copies in the first year. It made many people think that the abolitionists were right.

Not all abolitionists were northerners or slaves. Angelina and Sarah Grimké were from South Carolina. These two sisters freed the slaves on their own family's plantation. The sisters also traveled around the country speaking against slavery.

Harriet Beecher Stowe

Angelina Grimké   Sarah Grimké

Think About It

Many of the abolitionists lived in the North. Why was this so?

What would you do if you believed something was very wrong and wanted to change it?

Working on the Erie Canal

People in the South mostly continued to work as farmers. In the North, people had many more work opportunities, such as the Erie Canal. Laborers, carpenters, and masons built and later repaired the canal. Teamworkers drove the animals that pulled the ships along the canal.

The Erie Canal

— Erie Canal,
   built 1817-1825

— Other canals in New York,
   built by 1840

CANADA

Lake Ontario

Watertown

Lake Champlain

Oswego

OSWEGO CANAL

Oneida Lake

BLACK RIVER CANAL

Black R.

Rochester

Rome

Utica

CHAMPLAIN CANAL

Mohawk R.

Syracuse

Buffalo

NEW YORK

Schenectady

Troy

Lake Erie

Albany

GENESEE VALLEY CANAL

Finger Lakes

CHENANGO CANAL

Chenango R.

Hudson R.

Allegheny R.

Olean

Binghamton

0   25   50 mi.
0   25   50 km

▲ The Erie Canal was one of the major transportation routes in the North before the Civil War.

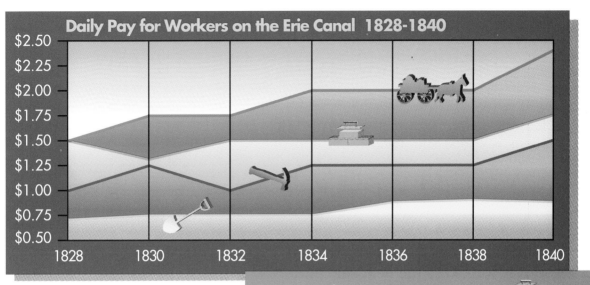

Daily Pay for Workers on the Erie Canal 1828-1840

	1828	1830	1832	1834	1836	1838	1840

(y-axis: $2.50, $2.25, $2.00, $1.75, $1.50, $1.25, $1.00, $0.75, $0.50)

CHART KEY

Laborers

Carpenters

Masons

Teamworkers

Write About It

Which group of workers was always paid the least?

Which group of workers earned $2.00 a day in 1834?

Which groups of workers saw their pay fall in some years?

Why do you think that teamworkers were paid more than other types of workers?

Harriet Tubman

Harriet Tubman was an escaped slave. She became famous because of her work on the Underground Railroad. The Underground Railroad wasn't really a railroad. It was a system that helped slaves travel to the North in secret and become free.

People in both the North and South hid escaped slaves during the day. At night, the slaves walked to the next safe place. The slaves kept walking north until they did not fear being caught and returned to their owners.

Harriet Tubman (far ▶ left) helped these people escape from slavery.

Tubman had escaped from slavery by using the Underground Railroad. But after her escape, she could not forget that her family was still living in slavery in the South. So she took great risks returning in secret often to the South to help others escape. Over the years, Tubman helped more than 300 people escape from slavery. For this, she is known as the most famous conductor on the Underground Railroad.

◀ This farm was a stop on the Underground Railroad.

Talk About It

What kind of people do you think helped African Americans escape from slavery?

Nobody Knows the Trouble I've Seen

*This song describes the feelings of many
African Americans before the Civil War.*

Nobody knows the trouble I've seen,
Nobody knows but Jesus.
Nobody knows the trouble I've seen,
Glory, Hallelujah!

Sometimes I'm up, sometimes I'm down,
Oh, yes, Lord;
Sometimes I'm almost to the ground,
Oh, yes, Lord.

Tell what you learned.

1. Have you ever traveled on a canal or a railroad? Tell about it.

2. Where were the differences between the North and South? How did they lead to conflict?

3. Why did Harriet Tubman risk her life again and again?

4. The abolitionists opposed slavery. What are some of the things that groups of people oppose today? How are these people like the abolitionists? How are they different?

6 War Between North and South

Tell what you know.

Wars affect many people besides soldiers. What do these pictures show about the effects of the Civil War?

Talk About It

Has a war ever affected
you or your family? How?

93

The Nation's Bloodiest War

Abraham Lincoln became President of the United States in 1861. His political party was against slavery in the new states. The southern states were afraid of this idea. So they **seceded**, or left, the United States. The southern states believed they had the right to leave. Lincoln and others thought that no state had this right.

The Civil War began in 1861 and ended in 1865. The North fought the South and the North won. It had more factories to make guns and uniforms. It had more railroads to move soldiers and supplies. When the war ended, all the slaves were freed.

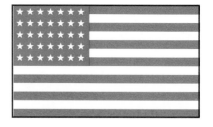

▲ Union flag (the North)

▲ Confederate flag (the South)

Both sides had thought that the war would be over quickly. People thought that few soldiers would be hurt. In fact, the Civil War was the nation's bloodiest war. About 618,000 Americans died in the war. Hundreds of thousands of others were wounded.

Think About It

In the Civil War, brothers fought against brothers and fathers fought against sons. What does this say about the beliefs held by both sides?

Leaders of the War

A Northern Leader

 Abraham Lincoln was born in a log cabin. His family was poor, but he worked hard, studied, and became a lawyer. He was honest, and people trusted him. In fact, they called him "Honest Abe."

As President, Lincoln led the United States through very difficult times. He believed that the nation would not survive if states could secede. He had said, "A house divided against itself cannot stand." Lincoln worked hard and kept the nation together. Many people think he was the nation's greatest President.

A Southern Leader

 Robert E. Lee was a wealthy army general from Virginia. When the war started, President Lincoln asked Lee to lead the northern troops. But Lee was a southerner. Lee felt it was not right to fight against his home state.

Lee led the southern troops during the war. He was a great general, but the North had more people, railroads, and other things needed to fight a war. After the war, Lee returned to his Virginia home. People in both the North and the South respected Lee as a great leader.

Talk About It

Lincoln said, "A house divided against itself cannot stand." How does this apply to your classroom? How does this apply to a family?

Famous People of the War

A War Photographer

Mathew Brady was one of the first photographers in the United States. He helped the world learn about the Civil War. Brady and his helpers traveled with the northern army. Their cameras were very heavy and hard to use, but they took about 7,000 photographs of the war. Today these photographs are famous. They are a major part of the record of the war.

▼ Mathew Brady (below) took many photographs of Abraham Lincoln.

Try It Out

Take photographs that describe your neighborhood. What things would you include? What things would you leave out? Why?

A Civil War Angel

In 1861, the northern and southern armies had few doctors, nurses, or supplies. A Massachusetts woman named Clara Barton changed that for the northern armies. She collected medical supplies and took them to battles. Her work helped thousands of wounded soldiers. She earned the respect of the nation. After the war, she founded the American Red Cross, a group that helps people in time of need.

Word Bank

brave

caring

hard-working

Write About It

What kind of person do you think Clara Barton was?

Tramp! Tramp! Tramp!

Many soldiers were taken prisoner and held in prison camps during the Civil War. This song talks about a captured northern soldier who hopes he will soon be set free.

Tramp! Tramp! Tramp! the boys are marching;
Cheer up, comrades, they will come.
And beneath the starry flag,
We shall breathe the air again,
Of the free land in our own beloved home.

When Johnny Comes Marching Home

This song was sung to southern soldiers at the start of the war. Many people then believed that the war would be short and wonderful.

When Johnny comes marching home again,
Hurrah! Hurrah!
We'll give him a hearty welcome then,
Hurrah, Hurrah!
Then men will cheer, and the boys will shout,
The ladies they will all turn out,
And we'll all feel gay,
When Johnny comes marching home!

Talk About It

These two songs tell about life in the United States during the Civil War. They have been sung for many years. Do you know any songs that tell about life in the nation where you were born or that have been sung there for many years?

Thunder at Gettysburg

by Patricia Lee Gauch

Introduction
This is the true story of Tillie Pierce, age 14. In July, 1863, the bloodiest battle in U.S. history took place at her hometown of Gettysburg, Pennsylvania. Tillie was looking for a safe place, but she got caught in the middle of the battle. She is with Henny, a neighbor woman, and Henny's two small girls. They have spent the night in the Weikert family's farm house where Tillie talked with a wounded northern soldier. Tillie supports the North.

NO RUMBLING / NO SHOOTING

July 3, 1863

First thing in the morning

Tillie took Mrs. Weikert's big blue cup

filled with steaming tea downstairs.

The soldier would like that,

she knew.

Tillie was happy to see him

still sleeping near the doorway.

"Sir!" she said quietly.

But he didn't move.

It was as if he were frozen.

"Sir?" Tillie said again, louder.

Her stomach started to hurt.

"General Weed's dead, miss,"

a soldier said.

"He died some time in the night."

The hurt wouldn't go away.

Reader's Tip
General Weed was the
soldier that Tillie had
talked to the night
before.

When the officers put the two cannons

on either side of the house

and told everyone to get to a safe place,

Tillie just followed everyone else

into the wagon.

She could hear the drums

rolling,

the fifes trilling,

and she could hear a low rumble

of voices like leaves in the wind

down Cemetery Ridge way.

But she rode silently,

down Taneytown Road, over the cross road,

toward Baltimore pike.

On the way she saw some prisoners.

They looked plain tired.

Not so bad or so awful

as plain tired.

A lot like General Weed had looked.

The wagon finally stopped

at a little gray farmhouse beyond the pike.

It was full,

packed like a chicken house.

It seemed as though all the farm folk

and wounded near the battleground

had fled there.

And more kept coming,

each telling what he had seen or heard.

Language Tip
Vocabulary
A *fife* is a small musical instrument. People play it by blowing into it and moving their fingers over holes.

Language Tip
Vocabulary
A *pike* is a kind of road.

Reader's Tip
The prisoners were southern soldiers.

Reader's Tip
Rebs are a short name
for the southern
soldiers. Yanks are
another name for the
northern soldiers.

Language Tip
Vocabulary
A copse is a group of
small trees.

"Well," said one, "all I saw was smoke,

billowing smoke,

but I heard there's some rebel general—

Picket they called him—

sweeping his men across Cemetery

Ridge like . . .

a giant wave.

I do believe nothing will stop those Rebs!"

"Maybe," another said.

"But did you see those Yanks

lining up behind that stone wall

on Cemetery Ridge,

like it was a fortress."

"I did!" a third man yelled out.

"And I saw a gunner there

in a copse of trees just firing

and firing."

A latecomer put in quietly,

"They were fighting hand to hand

when I saw them.

Hand to hand.

Thousands of 'em.

Thousands and thousands of American men,

fighting each other."

Strategy Tip
Stop and Think
The latecomer talks about Americans, not Rebs and Yanks. What point do you think the author is making?

Tillie burst out the back door.

The doctors were setting up straw mats

right outside for the wounded.

CONNECT LANGUAGE • SOCIAL STUDIES/LITERATURE

She caught up with Henny,

who was carrying water.

Tillie started carrying water, too.

Then she helped the farmer's wife

rip some linen for bandages.

Then she helped a nurse carry blankets.

After that she cut bread

and passed it to the men.

Finally Henny told her, "Sit

for a minute, Till!"

"No, ma'am," Tillie said.

She didn't want to,

and she wouldn't.

Strategy Tip
Understand Character
How was Tillie helping?
Why did she want to
continue to help?

Reader's Tip
At the time of the Civil War, many people in the United States went to church on Sunday morning and did not work. Sunday morning was a quiet time. What does the sudden silence mean?

Language Tip
Vocabulary
Dusk is the time in the early evening just before total darkness.

Even this far away the rumbling

went on and on as though it would finally

split the sky.

But near three o'clock

Tillie felt the air get still.

Sunday morning still.

There was no rumbling or shooting

or shouting.

Nothing.

Some folks started waiting

by the fence or over by the hill,

but the Weikerts and Tillie started

back to the farm.

A misty dusk was settling

when they walked into the yard,

but Tillie could see.

WEIKERT FARM

Wounded men,
their arms and legs broken
or bleeding or gone,
lay scattered all over the yard.
Like bits of cloth.

Strategy Tip
Picture the Scene
Tillie sees the wounded
and dying soldiers. As
you read, picture the
scene in the your mind.
The author includes the
scene to show how
terrible war is.

Strategy Tip
Understand Character
What do you think Tillie
was thinking about at
the end when she sat on
the grass? What did she
learn about war?

Near the barn. Under the trees.

Everywhere.

Many calling for help.

And behind them near the fence,

a growing pile of long pine boxes.

Coffins.

Nobody could speak. Not Mrs. Weikert

or Henny, not the girls. Not Tillie.

And then a soldier passed them at the well.

"We won!" he said. "General Lee and his Rebels

aren't in retreat yet,

but everyone's saying it's over.

We've won!"

Tillie sat down on the wet grass.

For a long time she sat and thought.

About General Weed's hand

on her arm,

about the men lying outside on the straw mats.

About the smoke, the screaming bullets, bursting shells,

about . . . this yard . . . now.

It was better to win.

But look what had happened.

Dear God, look what happened.

The Gettysburg Address

In November, 1863, President Lincoln spoke at the dedication of a cemetery for soldiers at Gettysburg, Pennsylvania. His speech is one of the most famous in U.S. history. Here is part of what he said:

The world will little note, nor long remember what we say here, but it can never forget what they [these soldiers] did here. It is for us the living, rather, to be dedicated here to the unfinished work which they who fought here have thus far so nobly advanced. . . . that this nation . . . shall have a new birth of freedom—and that government of the people, by the people, for the people, shall not perish from the earth.

Talk About It

What do you think the unfinished work was? How can people carry on that work today?

Tell what you learned.

CHAPTER 6

1. What have you learned about the Civil War from studying this unit?

2. What picture in the unit taught you the most about the Civil War? Why?

3. What can the story about Tillie Pierce teach us about war?

4. In this unit, you studied about several people who lived during the time of the Civil War. Which person would you most like to meet? What questions would you ask that person?

The Solar System

Tell what you know.

What is the solar system?

What would you see traveling in space?

When did people begin to explore space? Where have they been? What have they discovered?

Talk About It

Why do people want to travel in space?

117

The Sun

The Parts of the Solar System

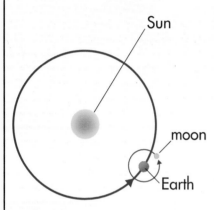

Sun

moon

Earth

The Sun is the center of the solar system. The Sun is a star. It produces light, heat, and energy. Nine planets **orbit,** or move around, the Sun. Earth is one of the planets that move around the Sun.

Other objects orbit the Sun. They are **asteroids** and **comets.**

Moons orbit planets, just as planets orbit the Sun. The Earth has one moon. Some planets have several moons.

Pluto

Comets are balls of rock and ice. The orbits of comets take them far from the Sun and then close to it. When a comet comes near the Sun, it warms up and forms a tail. Tails have been up to 200 million miles (320 million kilometers) long!

The solar system is vast. Thirty trips around the Earth are equal to one trip to the moon. One hundred trips to the moon are equal to one trip to Venus. Beyond the solar system, there are billions of stars and the rest of the universe.

Asteroids are pieces of rock and metal that orbit the Sun. The biggest asteroids are a few hundred miles or kilometers across.

Asteroid Belt

Mercury   Earth

Sun

Mars

Venus   Saturn

                    Neptune

Jupiter

Uranus

Talk About It

How are bodies in the solar system alike? How are they different?

What is the Sun like?

The Sun is a star much like other stars in the universe. It is a gigantic ball of burning gas. (**Gases** are materials like air that flow and do not have any shape.) The Sun produces energy. It produces a huge amount of light and heat.

The Sun is about 93 million miles (150 million kilometers) from the Earth. It takes 8 minutes and 20 seconds for the light from the Sun to travel to Earth. Very little of the heat and light from the Sun actually gets to Earth. It is lost in space.

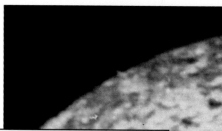

The Sun

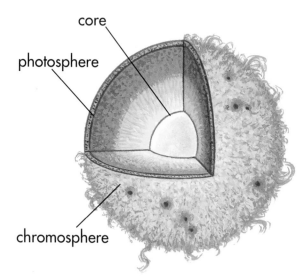

core

photosphere

chromosphere

core
The center of the Sun is made up of very hot gas. The temperature reaches about 27,000,000 degrees Fahrenheit (15,000,000 degrees Celsius). The core is like an exploding bomb. It produces the Sun's energy.

photosphere
This is the surface of the Sun. It is made of boiling gases. The temperature is about 10,000 degrees Fahrenheit (5,500 degrees Celsius). It gives off the Sun's energy as light and heat.

chromosphere
This is above the Sun's surface. It is made up of hot gases in motion. Gases often erupt, or burst out, from the Sun's surface into the chromosphere.

Compared to other stars, the Sun is medium-sized. Scientists classify it in the group of stars called **yellow dwarfs.** Yellow stars are not as hot as blue stars, but they are hotter than red ones.

The Sun's energy is produced at its center. This energy moves through the Sun's layers to its surface and out into space. The diagram on page 120 shows the main parts of the Sun.

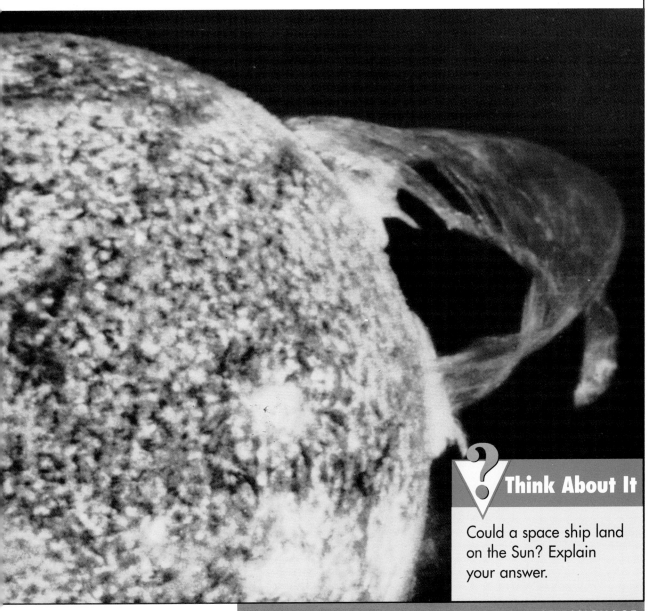

? Think About It

Could a space ship land on the Sun? Explain your answer.

Why does space look black?

When you see photographs of the planets in space, the space around the planets looks black. You can demonstrate why space looks dark.

Things You Need

 scissors cardboard box flashlight

Follow these steps.

1. Cut a small circle in one side of the cardboard box. Also cut a small hole in the top of the box for you to look through.

2. Turn out the lights in the room. Turn on the flashlight. Hold it over the hole at the side of the box.

3. Look through the hole in the top of the box. Where can you see the light?

You see a circle of light on the side of the box opposite the flashlight. You see little or no light between the flashlight and the side of the box.

Why is that? You can see light only when something reflects it into your eyes. The light reflects, or bounces, off the side of the box into your eyes. In the middle of the box, there is nothing for the light to bounce off.

There are very few things in space. So light passes through space and it is not reflected. That's why space looks dark.

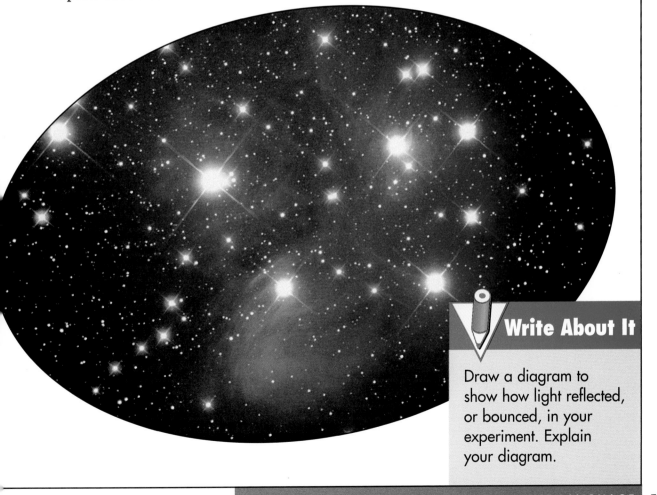

Write About It

Draw a diagram to show how light reflected, or bounced, in your experiment. Explain your diagram.

Ancient Ideas About the Universe

Ancient people knew that the Sun was important. It brought light and heat. Many peoples worshiped the Sun as a great and good god.

Ancient people told stories about the Sun. But the people of long ago did not know how the Sun really worked. They invented stories to explain why the Sun moved across the sky from east to west.

▲ The ancient Egyptians had a Sun god called Ra. They believed that when Ra crossed the sky in a boat, it was day.

▲ The ancient Greeks had a Sun god called Apollo. They believed that when he drove a chariot of fire across the sky, it was day.

Astronomers study the universe. Ancient peoples were the first astronomers. The ancient Greeks, for example, made maps of the stars. They gave names to the groups of stars that seem to form patterns in the sky. People still use these groups to talk about the stars.

The ancient Romans named the planets after their gods and goddesses. The names are still used in English. When scientists discovered three more planets in modern times, they named them after the Roman gods Uranus, Neptune, and Pluto.

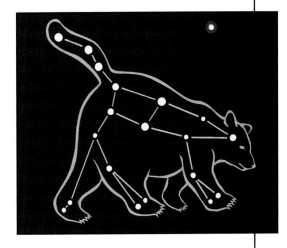

▲ One of the patterns that the Greeks saw in the stars was a big bear.

◀ The Romans named the largest planet after their most powerful god, Jupiter.

Talk About It

Do you know any stories about how the Sun, stars, or planets began? Share them with your classmates.

Here Comes the Sun

by George Harrison

Here comes the sun, here comes the sun,
And I say it's all right.
Little darling it's been a long cold lonely winter
Little darling it feels like years since it's been here.

Here comes the sun, here comes the sun,
And I say it's all right.

Little darling the smiles returning to their faces,
Little darling it seems like years since it's been here,

Here comes the sun, here comes the sun,
And I say it's all right.

Sun, sun, sun, here it comes.
Sun, sun, sun, here it comes.
Sun, sun, sun, here it comes.
Sun, sun, sun, here it comes.

Little darling I feel that ice is slowly melting,
Little darling it seems like years since it's been clear,

Here comes the sun, here comes the sun,
It's all right, it's all right.

Think About It

When the singer talks about the coming of the Sun, what season does he mean?

How does the Sun affect how the singer feels?

Does the Sun ever affect how you feel?

Brazilian Moon Tale

by Jane Yolen

Did you hear the one
about the moon
being nibbled, gnawed,
eaten away,
by a rat, a jaguar,
a lion, until
in one great gulp
it was gone?

I didn't believe it
either,
until I looked up
and saw that moon,
the teethmarks
still on it,
growing smaller every night.

Talk About It

Do you know any stories
that tell why the moon
grows smaller and
bigger in the sky? Share
them with your
classmates.

Tell what you learned.

1. Describe the parts of the solar system.

2. What is the most interesting fact you learned about the Sun?

3. How did ancient peoples' stories about the Sun relate to what they saw in the sky?

CHAPTER 8

The Planets

Word Bank

size

surface

temperature

spacecraft

telescope

Tell what you know.

What do you know about the planets?

How is Earth like other planets? How is it different?

How do people learn about the planets?

Talk About It

What planets interest
you the most? Why?

Facts About the Planets

The planets are in motion. They **revolve,** or orbit, the Sun. They also **rotate.** One rotation makes a complete day and a night.

The planets are different in many ways. Some planets are mainly rock with a metal core. Earth is one of these planets. Other planets are made mostly of gases. Each planet is surrounded by an **atmosphere** of gases. Earth's atmosphere is mainly oxygen. It holds in the heat from the Sun.

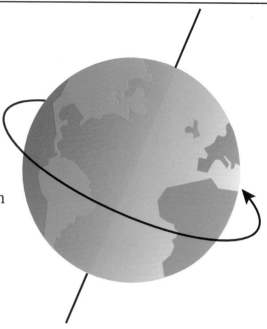

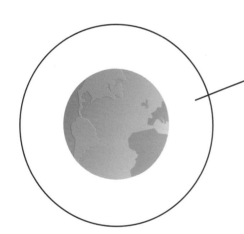

The Earth's atmosphere

Mercury is about the size of Earth's moon. Mercury has a rocky surface and a core of metal. Because it is so near the Sun, Mercury is very hot. Its temperature can reach 800 degrees Fahrenheit (427 degrees Celsius). It orbits the Sun quickly.

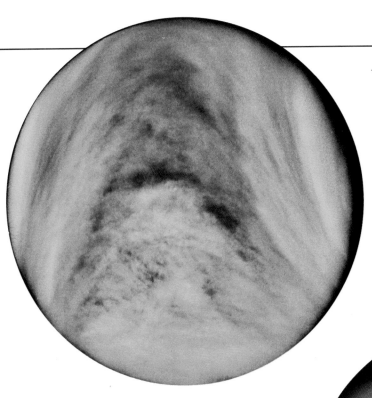

◀ Venus is almost the same size as Earth. Venus rotates very slowly. It takes 243 Earth days for Venus to rotate once. Venus seems to shine brightly in space because its thick clouds reflect sunlight.

Earth travels about 67,000 ▶ miles (107,200 kilometers) an hour in its orbit around the Sun.

◀ The surface of Mars is covered by orangish red soil. Wind blows the dusty soil around. The planet is very cold, and its atmosphere is thin.

Jupiter is a giant ball of gases. More than 1,000 Earths could fit inside it. Jupiter rotates very fast. A day is less than ten hours long. Swirls of clouds cover the planet. Jupiter has at least sixteen moons. Its biggest moon is bigger than Mercury.

Uranus has rings around it. It looks blue-green because of a gas in the clouds that cover the planet. Scientists think that there is rock and ice under the clouds. Uranus was discovered in 1781.

Pluto is the smallest and coldest planet. Astronomers guessed that Pluto existed before they first saw it in 1930. It is a cold ball of gas and rock. Some scientists think that it once was a moon of its neighbor, Neptune.

Planet	Length of One Rotation (in Earth time)	Length of One Orbit (in Earth time)
Mercury	59 days	88 days
Venus	243 days	224.7 days
Earth	24 hours	365.3 days
Mars	24.5 hours	687 days
Jupiter	9.8 hours	12 years
Saturn	10.7 hours	29.5 years
Uranus	17 hours	84 years
Neptune	16 hours	165 years
Pluto	6 days	248 years

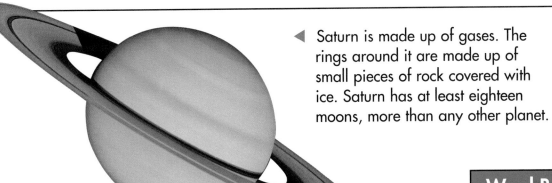

Saturn is made up of gases. The rings around it are made up of small pieces of rock covered with ice. Saturn has at least eighteen moons, more than any other planet.

Word Bank

gas

ring

solid

bigger

hotter

farther

more quickly

more slowly

Neptune looks blue because of a gas in its clouds. Strong winds blow across the planet at speeds of up to 1,240 miles (2,000 kilometers) an hour. Under the clouds are rock and ice. Neptune's moon, Triton, is one of the coldest places in the solar system.

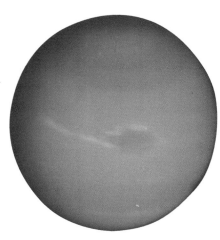

Average Temperature (Daytime)	Diameter at Its Center (km = kilometers)
662 ° F (350° C)	3,024 miles (4,878 km)
869° F (465° C)	7,504 miles (12,103 km)
59° F (15° C)	7,909 miles (12,756 km)
-9° F (-23° C)	4,207 miles (6,786 km)
-238° F (-150° C)	88,648 miles (142,980 km)
-292° F (-180° C)	74,735 miles (120,540 km)
-346° F (-210° C)	31,694 miles (51,120 km)
-364° F (-220° C)	30,709 miles (49,530 km)
-382° F (-230° C)	1,416 miles (2,280 km)

Write About It

Compare two planets. Write how they are alike and how they are different. Which one is bigger than the other? Which one is hotter than the other? Use the information in the captions and chart.

Space Exploration Time Line

People wanted to explore space for thousands of years. The time line shows what people have done in half a century of space exploration.

October 4, 1957 The Soviet Union started space flight with *Sputnik 1*, the first human-made satellite in space.

November 3, 1957 *Sputnik 2* went up with a dog named Laika.

1960

April 12, 1961 Soviet pilot Yuri Gagarin was the first person in space.

February 20, 1962 John Glenn was the first person from the United States to orbit the Earth.

July 20, 1969 *Apollo 11* landed on the moon. Neil Armstrong of the United States was the first person to walk on the moon.

1970

 Try It Out

The *Voyager 2* spacecraft is now traveling through space, beyond the solar system. It is carrying a special recording. The recording is a message to any other intelligent life in the universe. The recording has sounds from Earth, including music and the sound of a baby crying.

Work with a group. Prepare a tape recording of sounds that you would like to send to outer space.

April 19, 1971 The Soviets sent up *Salyut 1*, the first space station. People can live and work in a space station for long periods of time.

August 20, 1977 The United States sent up *Voyager 2* spacecraft. It took photographs of the outer planets in the solar system.

June 18, 1983 Sally Ride was the first woman from the United States in space.

1980

1990

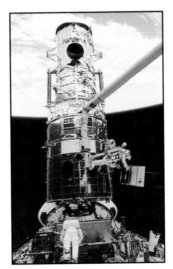

July 20, 1976 The U.S. *Viking* spacecraft landed on Mars and took pictures of its surface.

April 24, 1990 Europe and the United States sent up the Hubble space telescope. It is taking pictures of space as it orbits around Earth. It gets better pictures because it is above the atmosphere.

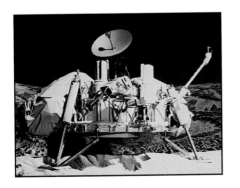

? Think About It

What should be the next thing we do in space? Should more people go up in space? Explain your choice.

How old would you be on Mars?

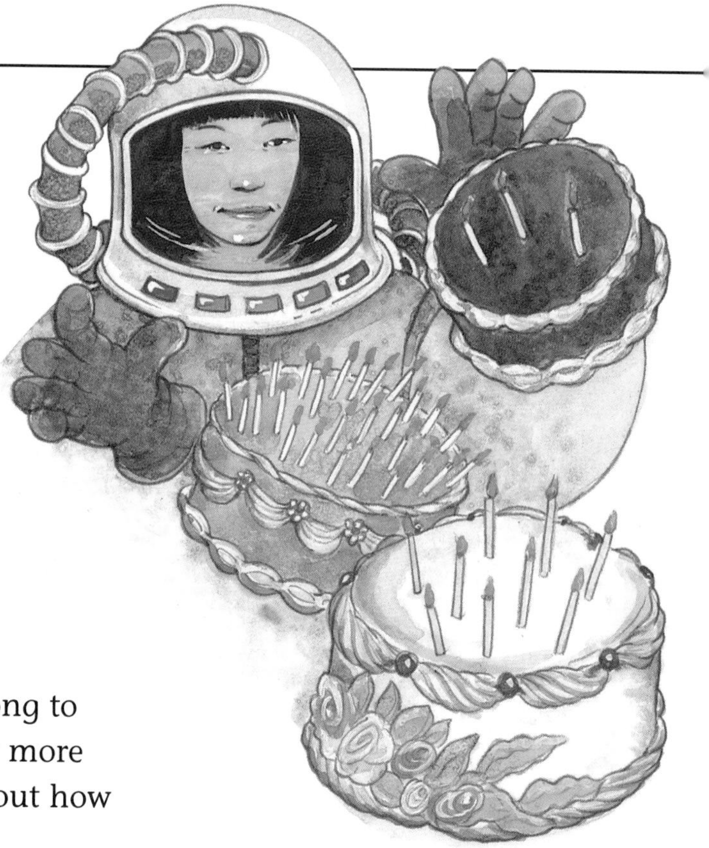

Years on other planets are longer or shorter than the years on Earth. A year is the amount of time it takes the planet to orbit the Sun. If you have a birthday every planet year, you would have more or fewer birthdays than you have on Earth.

The nearer planets don't take very long to orbit the Sun. You would have many more birthdays. Follow these steps to find out how old you would be:

1. Determine how many days you have lived on Earth. To do this, multiply your age by 365 days. Then add the number of days that have passed since your last birthday.

For example, if you are 13 years and 33 days old:
(13 X 365) + 33 = 4,778 Earth days old

2. Next use the chart below. Divide the number of days old you are by the number of days in the planet's year.

4,778
——————————————— = 54 years
88 (days in Mercury's year)

You would be **54 years old on Mercury!**

Planet	Length of Year in Earth Days
Mercury	88 days
Venus	225 days
Mars	687 days

The outer planets take much longer to travel around the Sun. You can calculate with years to find your age.

Divide your age by the number of Earth years it takes the planet to orbit the Sun.

For example, if you are 13 years old:

$$\frac{13}{29.5 \text{ years (for Saturn)}} = .44 \text{ year (or about 161 days)}$$

You wouldn't have had your first birthday yet on Saturn!

Planet	Length of Year in Earth Years
Jupiter	12 years
Saturn	29.5 years
Uranus	84 years
Neptune	165 years
Pluto	248 years

HAVE A LOT OF BIRTHDAYS FLY TO MERCURY

STAY YOUNG VISIT PLUTO

Think About It

Why are years longer on the planets farther from the Sun?

Where in the solar system would you like to have your birthday? Why?

The Solar System

by Maura Gouck

Language Tip
Vocabulary
A *meteor* is a piece of rock traveling in space. Usually meteors burn up when they enter the Earth's atmosphere.

On a clear, moonless night the sky seems to be filled with stars. Watch carefully, and you'll see that those twinkling stars are different colors—yellow, red, bluish white. You'll probably spot the *Big Dipper, Orion*, or another group of stars. If you are lucky, you might even see a meteor streaking across the sky!

Study Tip
Learn Key Vocabulary
This reading describes the solar system. Look for the key vocabulary you learned in this unit to understand the story more easily. When you read books in a subject area, it is helpful to keep a list of important words to remember.

As daylight arrives, the night stars fade from view. At sunrise there is only one star that you can still see. It is the star nearest to our planet. This star is the *Sun*. The Sun is very important because it provides light, heat, and energy to our planet.

To us, the Sun seems to be about the same size as the Moon, but it is really much larger. In fact, the Sun is about four hundred times wider than the Moon. The Sun is also much larger than our own planet Earth. It would take over one million Earths to fill the Sun!

You can't stare at the Sun the way you stare at other stars. The Sun is so bright it hurts your eyes. Scientists look at the Sun through special instruments. They see a lot happening on this star! To us the Sun looks like a peaceful, yellow disk floating slowly across the sky. Actually, though, it is a ball of bubbling, churning gases. Powerful storms swirl across its surface, and eruptions of hot gases shoot thousands of miles into space.

The Sun is the center of our *solar system*. The solar system consists of the Sun and the planets, asteroids, and comets that circle it. There are nine planets in our solar system. Each one follows a different path, or *orbit*, around the Sun.

The planet closest to the Sun is *Mercury*. It is a small planet, less than half the size of Earth. Mercury has a hard, rocky surface covered by many *craters*. Craters are circular holes formed when rocks, called *asteroids*, crashed into the planet. The temperature on Mercury ranges from very hot to icy cold. Humans could not survive on this planet because it has no water and very little air.

Strategy Tip
Read On to Get Meaning
The author uses a word you may not know, crater. When you read on, the author gives the meaning of the word. What is a crater?

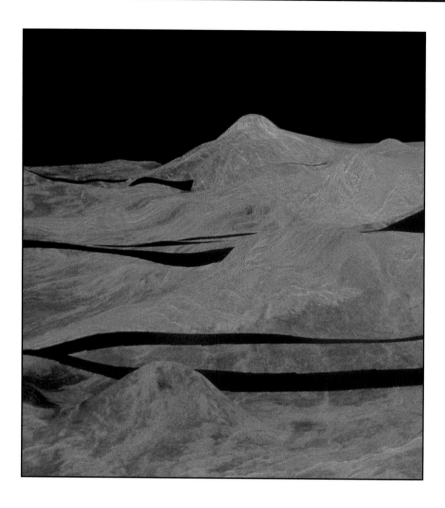

Strategy Tip
Understand
Comparisons
Authors often compare things you don't know with things you do know. The author uses the expression "hotter than a pizza oven" to help you understand how hot Venus is.

The hottest planet is *Venus*, the second planet from the Sun. The temperature on Venus is hotter than a pizza oven! Venus is about the same size as Earth. Sometimes these two are called sister planets, but they have really very little in common. Venus is covered by thick, yellow clouds—but they're not rain clouds. They're made of poisonous acid! Venus and Earth even spin in opposite directions. If you lived on Venus, you would watch the Sun rise in the west and set in the east!

We live on *Earth*, the third planet from the Sun. Earth is about 93 million miles from the Sun. It would take more than fifteen years to fly from Earth to the Sun in a jet plane!

Photographs taken from space show us that Earth is a beautiful blue ball surrounded by a layer of air—our *atmosphere*. The blue, of course, is caused by all the water in Earth's oceans. About three-fourths of Earth's surface is covered by water. Earth's water and air, along with light and heat from the Sun, make it possible for plants and animals to live. As far as we know, Earth is the only planet on which life exists.

Even Earth's nearest neighbor, the Moon, has no life. There is no water on the Moon and no air to breathe. Astronauts who landed there found a cratered landscape covered with gray, powdery dirt. The Moon is beautiful to look at from Earth, but you wouldn't want to live there!

Reader's Tip
To read about the rest of the planets, get the book *The Solar System* by Maura Gouck.

Exploring the Planets

Strategy Tip
Locate Places
This article describes the trip of the *Voyager 2* spacecraft. Use your knowledge about the order of the planets to follow the order in which they are described.

How do people learn about the planets? Of course, people have used telescopes for centuries. Modern-day telescopes are very powerful, but their ability to show the planets is still limited.

That's why over the last thirty years scientists have sent small spacecraft on trips to the planets to take close-up pictures. For example, spacecraft have landed on Venus and Mars and taken pictures of their surfaces.

The most interesting of all these spacecraft was *Voyager 2*. It was launched by the United States on August 20, 1977, to explore the outer planets. It took *Voyager* two years to reach its first destination, the planet Jupiter.

Voyager took pictures of Jupiter's clouds and measured their temperatures. But the most amazing pictures were the close-ups that Voyager took of Jupiter's moons. The icy moon Europa is the smoothest object in the solar system. Some people call Jupiter's moon Io a pizza pie because of its reddish-yellow colors. Voyager showed that Io had active volcanoes, mountains that throw out fiery gases.

The next destination was Saturn. There *Voyager* found eleven new moons. The most unusual may be Hyperion. Because so many objects have hit into it, it is not round.

Uranus was disappointing to the scientists. *Voyager* did find ten new moons circling the planet. But *Voyager* was not able learn much about Uranus because of the thick clouds that cover it.

Twelve years after its launch, *Voyager* reached its final destination, the planet Neptune. After Uranus, Neptune was a surprise. *Voyager* found stormy clouds moving around the planet. *Voyager* also proved that Neptune, like Jupiter, had rings.

Voyager explored Neptune's large moon, Triton. Voyager found several active volcanoes on Triton, but the volcanoes throw out water, not hot rock.

After *Voyager* passed Neptune, it left the solar system and entered outer space. It will continue sending information to Earth until about 2010.

Strategy Tip
Stop and Think
What does this article tell you about what scientists know about the planets? Why is it hard for scientists to get information about the planets?

Space Idioms

Here are some English idioms that have words related to space. Can you find the words?

To space out — to not pay attention, ▶
to be thinking about something else.
*"I'm sorry. Could you tell me that
address again? I spaced out while
you were talking."*

Sunny-side up — a way to cook an ▶
egg by frying it with the yolk-side up.
*"I like my eggs sunny-side up, with
wheat toast."*

▲ **Out of this world** — especially
wonderful or great.
"This pizza is out of this world!"

Sitting on top of the world — feeling ▶
very happy.
*"Jason has been sitting on top of the world
since he saw his good test scores."*

Tell what you learned.

1. How is the Earth like other planets in the solar system? How is it different?

2. Choose a planet you would most like to visit. Write a letter to the U.S. space organization NASA and tell why you want to travel there. Give two reasons.

3. Pick what you think is the most important event listed on the Space Exploration Time Line. Tell why you picked it.

4. What is the most interesting fact you learned about the planets? What other things would you like to learn about the planets?

A Growing Nation

The United States changed greatly during the 1800s and early 1900s. Many people moved to new homes in the West. New industries began. What do these pictures show about the United States during this time?

Word Bank

car

factory

farm

oil

wagon

Talk About It

How is life different for you now from what it was in the country where you were born?

155

CHAPTER 9

Settling the West

Settlers and Indians

Before 1800, most people in the United States lived in the area east of the Appalachian Mountains. During the 1800s, however, many thousands moved west. Eventually these **settlers** moved as far west as the Pacific coast.

American Indians had already lived in this huge area for thousands of years. As the settlers moved west, there were terrible wars between the settlers and the Indians. After years of fighting, the Indians were defeated and forced to live in areas the settlers did not want.

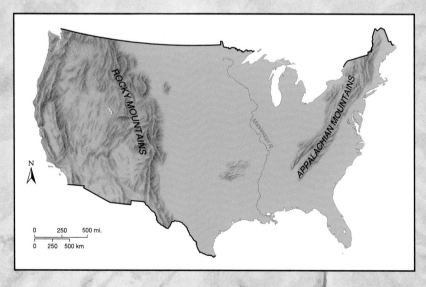

Many of the settlers had been born in Europe. Other settlers had been born in the East. However, most of these people had the same dream. They wanted a better life for their families and themselves. Most of all, the settlers wanted to own some land.

Many of the Europeans had been farmers. But their farms were too small or the soil was too poor to grow enough for their needs. Also, it was hard to buy good land. The Europeans hoped to start farms in the West. The settlers from the East wanted the same thing.

! Talk About It

What reasons did your family have for wanting to come to the United States? What dreams did you have before you got here? What dreams do you have now?

Getting and Settling the Land

The U.S. government gave land to people who had fought in the American Revolution or the War of 1812. The government also sold land to settlers. Sometimes, rich people bought big areas of land. Then they sold pieces of it to settlers at a profit.

Many settlers just moved onto open land and started farms and ranches. Later Congress and state governments passed laws saying that these settlers owned the land they had taken.

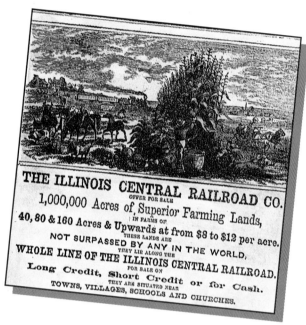

THE ILLINOIS CENTRAL RAILROAD CO.
OFFER FOR SALE
1,000,000 Acres of Superior Farming Lands,
IN FARMS OF
40, 80 & 160 Acres & Upwards at from $8 to $12 per acre.
THESE LANDS ARE
NOT SURPASSED BY ANY IN THE WORLD,
THEY LIE ALONG THE
WHOLE LINE OF THE ILLINOIS CENTRAL RAILROAD.
FOR SALE ON
Long Credit, Short Credit or for Cash.
THEY ARE SITUATED NEAR
TOWNS, VILLAGES, SCHOOLS AND CHURCHES.

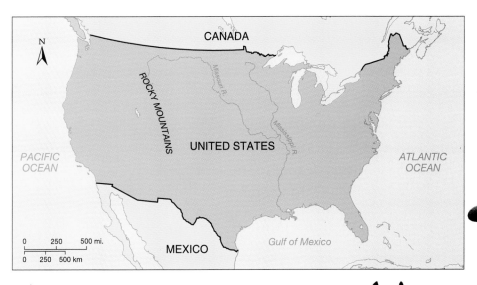

Settlers moved to almost all areas of the West. In the 1820s, people thought the area between the Missouri River and the Rocky Mountains was useless to farmers. Settlers thought they could not farm there because the land did not have forests, as the land had in their old homes. Instead, this huge flat area was **grasslands.** It looked like an ocean of waving grass and flowers. But by 1870, settlers had begun to turn this "useless" area into farms for raising wheat and corn and ranches for raising cattle and sheep.

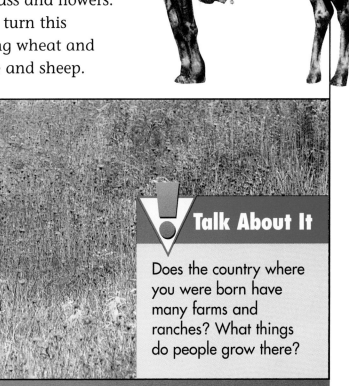

Talk About It

Does the country where you were born have many farms and ranches? What things do people grow there?

How did the settlers get to the West?

Early settlers often went west in Conestoga wagons. These large wagons had four big wheels and were pulled by horses or oxen. The wagon tops were covered with cloth to keep out the sun and rain. A family kept all its things in the wagon.

Most of the people in a family walked. Many times large groups of families and their wagons traveled together. This was called a **wagon train.** A wagon train traveled about 12 to 20 miles (19 to 32 kilometers) a day.

Try It Out

How far could you walk in one day if you walked for ten hours? Work with a partner. Walk at a slow pace for one minute down a school hall. Measure how many feet you walked. Multiply this by 60 to figure out how many feet you could walk in an hour. Then multiply by 10 hours to see how many feet you could walk in a day. Divide by 5,280 to get the number of miles.

On May 10, 1869, a **transcontinental railroad** was completed. This made it possible to travel across the continent, from New York to California, by railroad. Now travelers could cross the continent in just ten days. Cities and farms were started along the railroad. By 1893, four more major railroad lines crossed the continent.

Word Bank

airplane

boat

bus

car

ship

truck

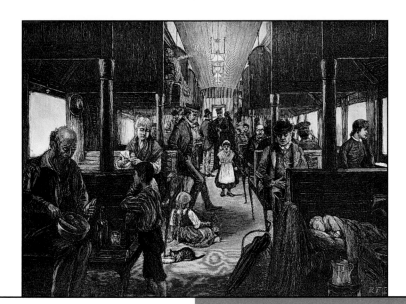

Write About It

Think of a time you moved to a new place. How did you get to the new place?

Biomes of the West: Grasslands and Forests

A **biome** is a region that has a certain kind of climate and certain animals and plants. The United States has a huge grasslands biome called the **prairie.** It has many kinds of grass, but only a few trees. The prairie usually gets little precipitation. Farmers now grow wheat, oats, and corn on the prairie. Before the time of the settlers, huge herds of buffalo lived on the prairie. But by 1885, buffalo hunters had reduced the total number from 60 million to about one thousand.

Settlers who moved beyond the prairie came
to a forest biome. A forest biome gets a lot of
precipitation. This makes it possible for many
kinds of plants and animals to live there.
A forest biome has many kinds of trees
such as maples and oaks. Deer, owls,
and beavers live in a forest biome.

Write About It

What kind of biomes
are there in the place
where you or your
parents were born? (If
you don't know, look in
books in the library for
the answer.)

Sarah, Plain and Tall

by Patricia MacLachlan

In this story, a farmer with two children has advertised for a wife. A woman named Sarah, from the state of Maine, has answered the ad. Sarah has agreed to come for a visit to see if she and the farm family can make a life together.

Reader's Tip
Settler families needed to be large to do all the work on a farm. It was important for a parent to marry again if a mother or father died. This other adult person was needed to do work.

Language Tip
Vocabulary
Indian paintbrush is a type of plant with red and orange flowers.

Sarah came in the spring. She came through green grass fields that bloomed with Indian paintbrush, red and orange, and blue-eyed grass.

Papa got up early for the long day's trip to the train and back. He brushed his hair so slick and shiny that Caleb laughed. He wore a clean blue shirt, and a belt instead of suspenders.

He fed and watered the horses, talking to them as he hitched them up to the wagon. Old Bess, calm and kind; Jack, wild-eyed, reaching over to nip Bess on the neck.

"Clear day, Bess," said Papa, rubbing her nose. "Settle down, Jack." He leaned his head on Jack.

And then Papa drove off along the dirt road to fetch Sarah. Papa's new wife. Maybe. Maybe our new mother.

Gophers ran back and forth across the road, stopping to stand up and watch the wagon. Far off in the field a woodchuck ate and listened. Ate and listened.

Caleb and I did our chores without talking. We shoveled out the stalls and laid down new hay. We fed the sheep. We swept and straightened and carried wood and water. And then our chores were done.

Study Tip
Understand Point of View
This story is told in the first person. This means that the story teller is also in the story. This style makes the story seem very real and personal.

Language Tip
Vocabulary
A *gopher* is a small, furry animal. A *woodchuck* is a larger furry animal that sleeps in a hole in the ground all winter.

Reader's Tip
Maggie is a neighbor
woman.

Caleb pulled on my shirt.

"Is my face clean?" he asked. "Can my face be too clean?" He looked alarmed.

"No, your face is clean but not too clean," I said.

Caleb slipped his hand into mine as we stood on the porch, watching the road. He was afraid.

"Will she be nice?" he asked. "Like Maggie?"

"Sarah will be nice," I told him.

"How far away is Maine?" he asked.

"You know how far. Far away, by the sea."

"Will Sarah bring some sea?" he asked.

"No, you cannot bring the sea."

The sheep ran in the field, and far off the cows moved slowly to the pond, like turtles.

"Will she like us?" asked Caleb very softly.

I watched a marsh hawk wheel down behind the barn.

He looked up at me.

"Of course she will like us." He answered his own question. "We are nice," he added, making me smile.

We waited and watched. I rocked on the porch and Caleb rolled a marble on the wood floor. Back and forth. Back and forth. The marble was blue.

We saw dust from the wagon first, rising above the road, above the heads of Jack and Old Bess. Caleb climbed up onto the porch roof and shaded his eyes.

Strategy Tip
Understand Character
Caleb keeps asking questions, and the story teller says he is afraid. Why is he afraid?

Language Tip
Vocabulary
A *bonnet* is a kind of
hat worn by women in
the 1800s.

"A bonnet!" he cried. "I see a yellow bonnet!"

The dogs came out from under the porch, ears up, their eyes on the cloud of dust bringing Sarah. The wagon passed the fenced field, and the cows and sheep looked up, too. It rounded the windmill and the barn and the windbreak of Russian olive that Mama had planted long ago. Nick began to bark, then Lottie, and the wagon clattered into the yard and stopped by the steps.

"Hush," said Papa to the dogs.

And it was quiet.

Sarah stepped down from the wagon, a cloth bag in her hand. She reached up and took off her yellow bonnet, smoothing back her brown hair into a bun. She was plain and tall.

"Did you bring some sea?" cried Caleb beside me.

"Something from the sea," said Sarah, smiling. "And me." She turned and lifted a black case from the wagon. "And Seal, too."

Carefully she opened the case, and Seal, gray with white feet, stepped out. Lottie lay down, her head on her paws, staring. Nick leaned down to sniff. Then he lay down, too.

"The cat will be good in the barn," said Papa. "For mice."

Sarah smiled. "She will be good in the house, too."

Sarah took Caleb's hand, then mine. Her hands were large and rough. She gave Caleb a shell—a moon snail, she called it—that was curled and smelled of salt.

"The gulls fly high and drop the shells on the rocks below," she told Caleb. "When the shell is broken, they eat what is inside."

"That is very smart," said Caleb.

"For you, Anna," said Sarah, "a sea stone."

And she gave me the smoothest and whitest stone I had ever seen.

"The sea washes over and over and around the stone, rolling it until it is round and perfect."

"That is very smart, too," said Caleb. He looked up at Sarah. "We do not have the sea here."

Sarah turned and looked out over the plains.

"No," she said. "There is no sea here. But the land rolls a little like the sea."

Reader's Tip
What do you think will happen? Will Sarah stay? To find out, read the rest of the book, Sarah, Plain and Tall.

Home on the Range

*Many of the settlers wanted a better life. This song
talks about their hopes and the beautiful
countryside some believed they had found.*

Oh, give me a home where the buffalo roam,
Where the deer and the antelope play;
Where seldom is heard a discouraging word,
And the skies are not cloudy all day.

Home, home on the range,
Where the deer and the antelope play;
Where seldom is heard a discouraging word,
And the skies are not cloudy all day.

Talk About It

What words in the song
talk about the hope that
settlers had for their lives
on the prairie?

Tell what you learned.

1. How is travel today easier than it was for the settlers in the 1800s?

2. What do you think were the good parts of being a settler in the West during the 1800s? What were the bad parts?

3. If you could choose, would you rather live in a grassland biome or a forest biome? Why?

4. If you were a settler going west in the 1800s, what things would you bring with you? What would you leave behind?

5. What did you learn about life in the West from the story *Sarah, Plain and Tall?*

CHAPTER 10

Industry Changed the Nation

Word Bank

camera

car

electric light

telephone

typewriter

Tell what you know.

All these things were invented in the
United States in the 1800s and early 1900s.
How do they affect our lives today?

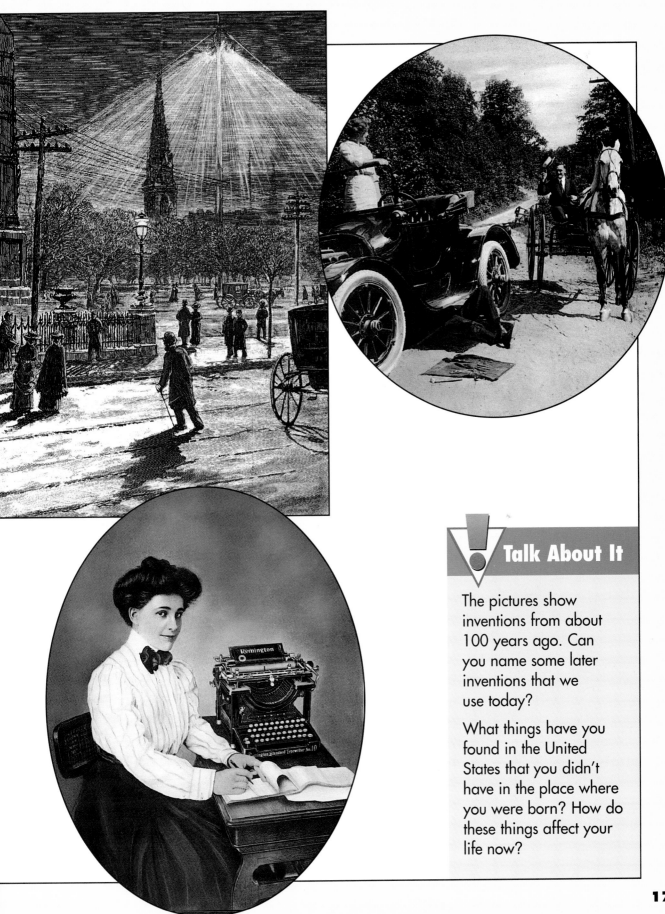

The pictures show inventions from about 100 years ago. Can you name some later inventions that we use today?

What things have you found in the United States that you didn't have in the place where you were born? How do these things affect your life now?

The Industrial Revolution

During the 1800s, the United States changed greatly. Thousands of people left farms, ranches, and small towns to work in factories in the cities. These changes took place because of the Industrial Revolution.

Before the 1800s, there were few factories. People made things by hand at home or in small shops. Then inventors figured out how to use coal and oil to run machines. The number of factories grew quickly. Suddenly, there were more things to buy. There were faster ways to get places. There were new, easier ways of living.

These changes also caused problems. Working in early factories was hard and dangerous. Many workers were not treated well. Many people worked about twelve hours a day, six days a week. They lived in crowded, dark apartments. They often died at young ages. Children worked too. Some did dangerous jobs in coal mines and factories where adults were too large to go.

? Think About It

The United States now has laws about how many hours a day people can work. It also has laws about what is the lowest amount people can be paid. Do you think these are good laws or not? Why?

The Nation's Industrial Leaders and Inventors

The United States was the home of many inventors and industrial leaders in the 1800s and early 1900s. John D. Rockefeller started a giant company called Standard Oil. It sold oil to use in lamps. Later, it sold gasoline to run cars.

Henry Ford figured out a system to build cars quickly and cheaply. Before this time, only rich people could afford cars. Ford's system is called the **assembly line**. In this system, workers repeated the same job all day. A worker might tighten the same part on many cars, one after another. This was possible because the parts were exactly alike.

Alexander Graham Bell was an immigrant from Scotland. He invented the telephone in 1876. By 1900, there were over 1.5 million telephones in the United States.

◄ Many leaders of this time were friends. This picture shows Henry Ford, Thomas Edison, U.S. President Warren G. Harding, and Harvey Firestone on vacation together in the early 1920s. Firestone's company made car tires.

PROF. THAD SHERIDAN FRITZ'S

PHONOGRAPH FESTIVAL

Thomas A. Edison.

THE

WONDERFUL TALKING INVENTION

UNDER THE AUSPICES OF THE

OHIO LECTURE BUREAU.

In 1877, Thomas Edison invented both the microphone and the phonograph. In 1879, he invented the light bulb. In 1891, he invented the motion picture camera. He invented so many things that people called him the Wizard of Menlo Park, the New Jersey town where he lived.

Talk About It

How do we use electricity today? How would our lives be different if we did not have electric lights?

Why do you think most of the inventors and industrial leaders at this time were men?

Bringing Reform

By the early 1900s, many people thought that some things about business and industry needed to be changed. One of these people was Ida Tarbell. She wrote about John D. Rockefeller and his company. She told how he had forced some companies out of business and how he got unfair deals from others. She said Rockefeller's giant company was too powerful.

Because of Tarbell's writings, Congress passed some laws. Rockefeller had to break up his company into several smaller ones. Some business methods Rockefeller had used were made illegal.

Upton Sinclair wrote about the meat packing business. He showed that food being sold to people was dangerous to eat because it was not prepared safely. Because of Sinclair's book, the government made new rules about how food could be handled. This made food safe for everybody.

? Think About It

Today the U.S. government makes safety rules about medicines, cars, and working conditions. Do you think this is a good idea? Why or why not?

What does *reform* mean?

Charting Changes

The U.S. government gives patents to inventors. A patent says that the inventor is the only one who can make and sell the invention. In 1790, the U.S. government issued only 3 patents. In 1890, the government issued 28,304 patents. Study the graph. Why do you think the number of patents increased?

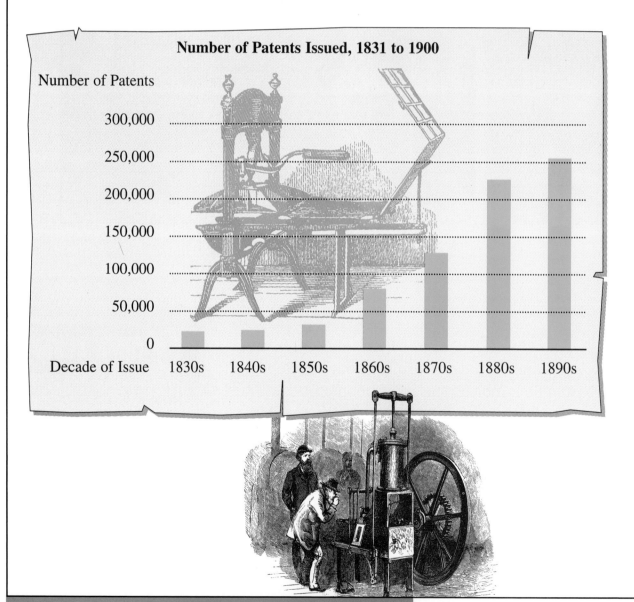

Number of Patents Issued, 1831 to 1900

Number of Patents

300,000
250,000
200,000
150,000
100,000
50,000
0

Decade of Issue   1830s   1840s   1850s   1860s   1870s   1880s   1890s

In the early 1800s, few Americans lived in urban areas or cities. Most people lived in rural areas of farms, ranches, and small towns. This began to change greatly after the U.S. Civil War. Study the graph. What does it tell you about life in the United States?

Americans Living in Rural and Urban Areas, 1870 to 1900

Percent

Rural

Urban

Year   1870   1880   1890   1900

Write About It

During which decade were the fewest patents issued?

What does the growth in the number of patents issued say about life in the United States during the 1800s?

Have you ever invented something? What was it?

What does the line graph tell us about where Americans were choosing to live? How can you explain this?

Do you live in an urban or a rural area now? What kind of area did you or your family live in in your native land?

Andrew Carnegie

by *William Jay Jacobs*

Andrew Carnegie lived from 1835 to 1919.
He is one of America's most famous immigrants.

If you knew that every month for the rest of your life you would receive at least $1 million, what would you do with the money?

In 1901 Andrew Carnegie sold his giant Carnegie Steel Company. Interest from his share of the sale price would bring him no less than $1 million a month, for life. What did he do with the money? He gave it all away! Indeed, during the last eighteen years of his life he gave away nearly $350 million.

The lives of rich men, said Carnegie, are divided into two parts. The first part is for getting money. The second should be for giving it away. . . .

Andrew Carnegie did not always have money to give away. In 1848, at the age of thirteen, he came to America from Scotland. He came with his father, mother, and younger brother, Thomas. His mother borrowed the money from friends to pay for their passage. In Scotland times were so hard that Andrew's father could find no work.

Young Carnegie's first job in America was in a cotton mill near Pittsburgh. . . .

SCOTLAND

PENNSYLVANIA
Pittsburgh

By the year 1900, he was master of the United States steel industry. He could make steel at lower cost than anyone in America or Europe. He had helped establish the United States as the largest producer of steel in the world. And it was steel that made the United States the leader among all the world's industrial nations.

▼ In 1872, Carnegie decided to enter the steel business.

Just then—at the peak of his success—Andrew Carnegie retired. In 1901 he sold all of his properties to J. Pierpont Morgan and a group of men who had founded the United States Steel Corporation. The sale price was almost half a billion dollars. After signing the papers Carnegie turned to Morgan with a sigh of relief. "Well, Pierpont," he said, "I am now handing the burden over to you."

For nearly twenty years afterward, Carnegie did the things he most enjoyed. He read, traveled, listened to fine music, collected art, wrote books about his ideas—and gave away money.

▲ J.P. Morgan

▲ The Carnegie Hero Fund Commission makes awards for bravery.

▲ Some of Carnegie's money was used to build Carnegie Hall in New York City. It is a famous concert hall.

Songs of the Industrial Revolution

The Erie Canal

*The Erie Canal was a major transportation route of
the 1820s and 1830s. Mules walked on the shore
and pulled the boats and barges on the canal.*

I've got a mule. Her name is Sal,
Fifteen miles on the Erie Canal.
She's a good old worker and a good old pal,
Fifteen miles on the Erie Canal.
We've hauled some barges in our day,
Filled with lumber, coal, and hay,
And we know every inch of the way
From Albany to Buffalo.

Low bridge, everybody down!
Low bridge, for we're coming to a town!
And you'll always know your neighbor,
You'll always know your pal,
If you ever navigated on the Erie Canal.

I've Been Working on the Railroad

Thousands of people worked long hours in all kinds of weather to build the transcontinental railroad. Many of these workers were immigrants from Ireland and China.

I've been working on the railroad,
All the live-long day,
I've been working on the railroad,
Just to pass the time away.
Don't you hear the whistle blowing,
Rise up so early in the morn;
Don't you hear the captain shouting,
"Dinah, blow your horn!"

▲ Chinese immigrants did some of the most dangerous jobs, such as building the tunnels for the transcontinental railroad.

In the 1930s, America went through hard economic times. People lost their jobs, and there weren't many new jobs. This song tells about the difficulties experienced by some workers during those years.

Once I built a railroad, I made it run
I made it run against time
Once I built a railroad, now it's done
Brother, can you spare a dime?

Once I built a tower, up to the sun
Bricks and mortar and lime
Once I built a tower, now it's done
Brother, can you spare a dime?

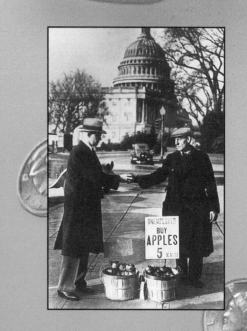

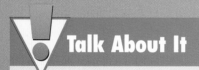

Talk About It

What two jobs did these workers once have? Why don't they have those jobs any more?

Tell what you learned.

1. How did life in the United States change between 1800 and 1900? What new kinds of jobs did people have by 1900?

2. Have you ever visited a factory? What was made there? Do you think it was dangerous or safe to work there? Why?

3. Many people say that the United States is going through another revolution of information and machines such as computers. What do you think they mean by this?

4. Would you rather live in a rural or in an urban area? Why?

Citizenship and Government

Word Bank

fairness

opportunity

freedom

Tell what you know.

What does the United States mean to you?

What do these pictures tell about the United States?

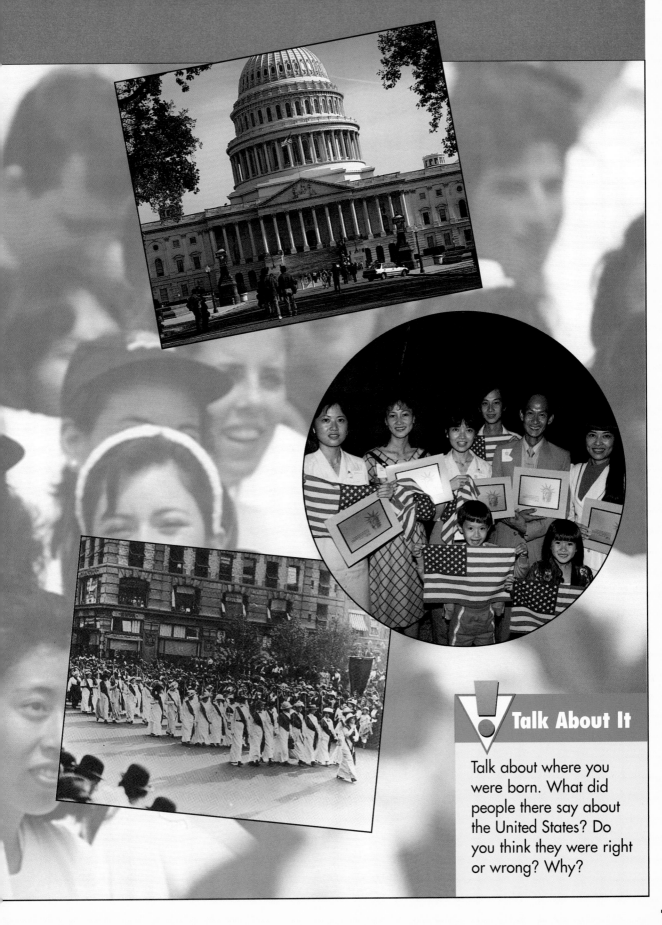

Talk About It

Talk about where you were born. What did people there say about the United States? Do you think they were right or wrong? Why?

CHAPTER 11

Citizenship

All Are Equal

A **citizen** is a person who is a member of a nation. A person can be a citizen by being born in a place. A person can also become a citizen by choosing to live in a place. About 250 million people live in the United States. More than 225 million of these people are citizens. Most of these people were born in the United States. They are citizens for that reason.

Many other citizens chose the United States as their home. They began life in some other country, and they came to the United States as immigrants. After living here for five years, they can become citizens.

Many immigrants become citizens because, in the United States, all people are equal before the law. This means that all people must be treated the same. This **equality** before the law is an important reason that many immigrants want to become citizens.

Write About It

Why did your family immigrate to the United States? Why did other people you know immigrate?

Becoming a Naturalized Citizen

Some U.S. citizens were born in other countries. These people are called **naturalized citizens.** They came to the United States and chose to become citizens here.

People who want to become U.S. citizens must do certain things and follow certain rules. People who want to become U.S. citizens must:

- live in the United States for 5 years
- be at least 18 years old
- be able to read, write, and speak some English
- know some of the history of the United States and something about the U.S. government
- be willing to support the United States above all other nations

▲ In 1940, scientist Albert Einstein became a U.S.citizen.

Try It Out

Pretend you are going to start your own country. Make up a set of rules for people who want to become citizens. Give a reason why each rule is important to the success of your new country.

People who want to become U.S. citizens must fill out papers that tell about themselves. They must go to a meeting with a government officer. At this meeting, they have to answer questions in English about U.S. history and government. They must swear to support the United States. When people have done all these things, they can become naturalized citizens of the United States.

Think About It

Do you think it is too hard or too easy to become a citizen of the United States? Why?

Being a Good Citizen

Citizens of the United States have many rights. They also have some responsibilities.

Voting is a basic responsibility of all adult citizens. The United States is a democracy. People choose their leaders by voting. Being a good citizen means voting in elections.

Another responsibility of all people in the United States, including citizens, is to obey the laws of the nation. It means paying taxes on time. It means being on a jury, and telling the truth in court.

A third responsibility is to be interested in the needs of your area. It means writing to elected officials about issues you feel are important. It means helping to raise money for new library books. It means helping neighbors in need.

Being a good citizen also means believing in fairness and respecting the rights of others. Only by being fair and respecting the rights of others can people expect to be treated that way themselves.

Word Bank

caring

fair

helpful

involved

respectful

responsible

▲ Good citizens help each other when disaster strikes.

Talk About It

Why do you think it is important to be a good citizen?

What words do you think describe a good citizen?

Facts About Immigration

Some decades have been times of great immigration. Other decades have not. Study the chart and answer the questions.

Immigration to the United States, 1900 to 1990	
Decade	Number of People
1900s	8,795,386
1910s	5,735,811
1920s	4,107,209
1930s	528,431
1940s	1,035,039
1950s	2,515,479
1960s	3,321,677
1970s	4,493,314
1980s	7,338,062

The number of immigrants from different continents has changed over time. To understand these changes, study the chart. Then answer the questions.

Where Immigrants Came From, 1820 to 1990		
Continent	1820 to 1940	1820 to 1990
Europe	32,468,776	37,045,140
Asia	1,074,926	6,098,449
The Americas	4,401,466	13,033,251
Africa	26,060	349,464

Talk About It

During which decade did the United States have the greatest immigration?

The 1930s were years of hard economic times. How does this chart show that things were not good in the United States then?

Which continent has provided the greatest number of immigrants?

The Statue of Liberty and Ellis Island

For people around the world, the Statue of Liberty is a symbol of the United States. For many years, the Statue of Liberty was the first thing many immigrants saw when they reached the United States. To them, it represented what they hoped to find here: fairness, equality, opportunity, and freedom.

In 1876, the United States was 100 years old. The people of France sent a gift to the people of the United States in honor of that anniversary. The gift was a giant statue that is known as the Statue of Liberty. The statue was put up on a tiny island in New York harbor.

A poem appears on the base of the Statue of Liberty. The poem was written by Emma Lazarus. Part of the poem says:

Give me your tired, your poor,
Your huddled masses yearning to breathe free,
The wretched refuse of your teeming shore.
Send these, the homeless, tempest-tost to me,
I lift my lamp beside the golden door!

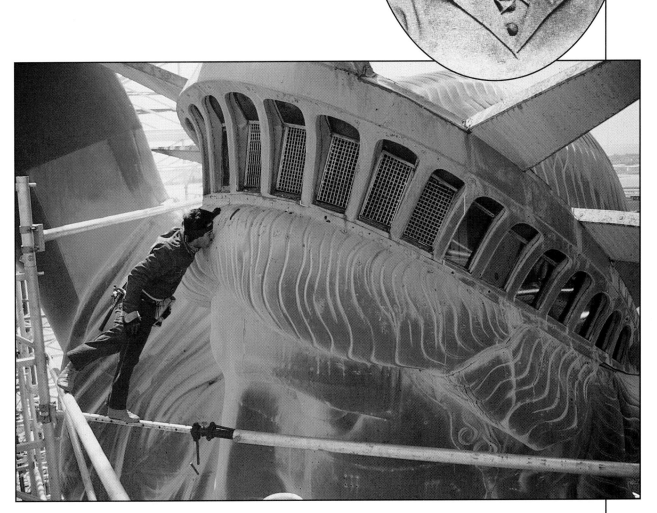

▲ The Statue of Liberty was cleaned and repaired in the 1980s.

Ellis Island is also in New York harbor, near the Statue of Liberty. Between 1892 and 1954, about 15 million immigrants entered the United States through Ellis Island. Most of them were poor people from Europe. They had sailed across the Atlantic Ocean.

Most people spent less than one day at Ellis Island. Government doctors quickly checked to see if they were sick. Only people with tuberculosis, leprosy, and a few other diseases were not allowed to enter the United States. The immigrants were interviewed for about two minutes each. If they had a little money, someplace to go, and someone to help them find work, they were free to enter.

▲ Ellis Island had a special playground for small children.

Today, Ellis Island is a museum. Visitors can tour the huge waiting room. They can see some of the things immigrants left behind and view other exhibits.

Think About It

Emma Lazarus used the words "golden door" in her poem. What do those words mean to you?

Why do you think the government wanted to be sure that immigrants had a little money and someplace to go?

Immigrants who passed through Ellis Island had crossed the Atlantic Ocean the cheapest way possible. The few rich immigrants often had better ship accommodations. They were examined on their ships. Do you think this was fair? Why or why not?

Coming to America: Letters from Rifka

by Karen Hesse

Introduction

This story is about a 13-year-old girl named Rifka who has traveled across the Atlantic Ocean alone to the United States in 1920. Her family had to leave her behind in Europe because she was sick. When she was well, she had to go on by herself. Now she is writing to her cousin Tovah who stayed behind in Russia. Rifka tells Tovah she soon expects to meet her older brothers who left for the United States so long ago that Rifka does not remember them.

October 1, 1920
Entering New York Harbor

Dear Tovah,

Today we will arrive at Ellis Island. Today I will see Mama and smell her yeasty smell. Today I will feel the tickle of Papa's dark beard against my cheeks and see my brother Nathan's dimpled smile and Saul's wild curly hair. Today I will meet my brothers Asher and Isaac and Reuben.

Reader's Tip
Rifka says she doesn't remember some of her brothers. What does this fact say about travel and life at that time?

Language Tip
Vocabulary
Baldness means having no hair. Rifka's hair had fallen out when she was sick.

Language Tip
Vocabulary
A *tallis* is a Jewish prayer shawl. A *locket* is a piece of jewelry that has a little picture in it. A locket is usually worn on a chain around the neck.

Study Tip
Use of the First Person
An author that writes a story using *I, my, me, we,* and *us* is telling the story in the first person. This author has Rifka tell the story in the first person in a letter. How does the writing style make you feel about what has happened to Rifka? Look for the use of the first person point of view when you read other stories.

Already I am wearing my best hat, the black velvet with the shirring and the brim of light blue. I'm hoping that with the hat, Mama will not mind my baldness. I've tucked Papa's tallis into my rucksack, but Mama's gold locket hangs around my neck.

The captain said his company notified our families and they are awaiting our arrival. I must pass a screening on the island before I can go home with Mama and Papa. Papa wrote about Ellis Island in his letters.

He wrote that at Ellis Island you are neither in nor out of America. Ellis Island is a line separating my future from my past. Until I cross that line, I am still homeless, still an immigrant. Once I leave Ellis Island, though, I will truly be in America.

Language Tip
Time
Rifka is talking about several different time periods in this letter. The way to figure out what happened first, next, and last is to study the verb tenses.

Strategy Tip
Understand Character
Is Rifka worried about answering questions at Ellis Island? Why or why not? What words in her letter tell you how she feels?

Papa said in his letter that they ask many questions at Ellis Island. I must take my time and answer correctly. What's to worry? I am good at answering questions. Even if they ask me a thousand questions, I will have Mama and Papa near me, my mama and papa.

Just one week ago, I did not think I would ever make it to America. We drifted on the sea for days, helpless, waiting for the ship to come and tow us. I assisted with the cleanup as best I could, doing work Pieter would have done if he were there.

Strategy Tip
Recognize Feelings
Imagine what Rifka must be feeling as she describes the trip across the ocean. Look for clues in Rifka's words.

Reader's Tip
Pieter is a young man Rifka met on the boat. He drowned in the storm that caused the ship to drift.

Then, once the tow ship arrived it took so long between the securing of the ropes and the exchanges between the two ships, I thought we would never begin moving. At last, when we did, the other ship pulled us so slowly. I could swim faster to America.

In Russia, all America meant to me was excitement, adventure. Now, coming to America means so much more. It is not simply a place you go when you run away. America is a place to begin anew.

In America, I think, life is as good as a clever girl can make it.

Very soon, Tovah, I will be in this America. I hope someday you will come, too.

Shalom, my cousin,

Rifka

P.S. As I was finishing this letter a cry went up from the deck. When I went out to see what it was, I found all the passengers gathered on one side of the ship, looking up. They were looking at Miss Liberty, Tovah, a great statue of a woman standing in the middle of the harbor. She was lifting a lamp to light the way for us.

Language Tip
Abbreviations
The initials *P.S.* stand for postscript. This abbreviation is sometimes used at the very end of a letter to indicate an idea or thought that the letter writer had after the letter was finished.

America the Beautiful

by Katharine Lee Bates

Katharine Lee Bates, a college professor, wrote the words to this famous song in 1893, just a year after Ellis Island had opened. Although Bates was not an immigrant, her words express the sentiments of many who are. Bates was inspired to write these words when she saw the spectacular view from Pikes Peak in Colorado during a visit there.

O beautiful for spacious skies,
For amber waves of grain,
For purple mountain majesties
Above the fruited plain.
America!
America!
God shed His grace on thee,
And crown thy good with brotherhood
From sea to shining sea.

Tell what you learned.

CHAPTER 11

1. What are some of the things a person must do to become a naturalized citizen?

2. Only about 2 percent of immigrants were turned away at Ellis Island. Still, many immigrants were fearful about the exams there. Why do you think this was so?

3. What facts that you learned about immigrants were the most interesting? Why?

4. The Statue of Liberty is a symbol of the United States. What symbols do you know of from the place where you were born?

CHAPTER 12

Government

Tell what you know.

The United States is a democracy.
Its government is of the people,
by the people, and for the people.
What do these pictures tell you
about the United States
government?

Word Bank

communism

democracy

dictatorship

monarchy

Talk About It

What kind of government was there in the place where you were born?

217

A Government of Laws

A **constitution** is a list of the basic laws and principles of a group. The Constitution of the United States is the world's oldest written constitution. It is the general plan for the organization and operation of the government of the United States. Because of the Constitution, the United States is governed by the rule of law. Nobody is above the law. All laws in the nation must agree with the Constitution.

▲ Men from each state approved and signed the Constitution on September 17, 1787.

People can see the signed copy of the Constitution in ▲
Washington, D.C.

The Constitution describes the organization of
the national government. The Constitution tells
what powers the national government has. The
Constitution says what powers are to be shared
by the national and state governments. The
Constitution also says what powers belong only
to the state governments.

In 1791, the first ten **amendments,** or changes
to the Constitution, were approved. These ten
amendments are called the Bill of Rights. The
Bill of Rights says that people have religious and
political freedom. It says that people have the
right to a trial in front of a jury.

Think About It

Why should citizens of
the United States learn
about the Constitution?

The Three Branches of Government

The Constitution of the United States divides the national government into three **branches**, or parts. These three branches make for a **separation of powers** so that no one person or group can get to be too powerful.

The **legislative** branch is the first branch. The legislative branch is the U.S. Congress. It makes the laws of the nation. The Congress meets every year in Washington, D.C.

The Congress has two parts: the House of Representatives and the Senate. The Senate has 100 members. Two members are elected from each state. Senators are elected for six-year terms.

The House of Representatives has 435 members. They are elected for two-year terms. The number of representatives from each state is determined by the state's population. Every state has at least one representative. California, the state with the largest population, gets 52 representatives.

The **executive** branch is the second branch. It is headed by the President of the United States. The President is elected for a four-year term. The President lives in the White House in Washington, D.C. The President approves the laws made by Congress. The President is commander in chief of the armed forces. The President deals with foreign governments. The President carries out the laws made by Congress and other duties.

▲ George Washington was the first President of the United States.

Executive Branch – Enforces laws

The System of Checks and Balances

Legislative Branch – Makes laws

Judicial Branch – Interprets laws

The **judicial** branch is the third branch of government. The judicial branch is the national court system of the country. The Supreme Court is the highest court. Its main job is to decide if laws or actions by government officials are allowed by the Constitution. The court has nine members. The President chooses them, and the Senate votes to approve them. The nine members are appointed for life.

Think About It

In the 1980s, California had 45 representatives. In the 1990s, California has 52 representatives. What does this tell about the population of California?

Some people say that the President is the most powerful person in the world but also has the hardest job in the world. What do you think they mean by this?

Amending the Constitution

The Constitution has been in use for more than 200 years. During all that time, there have been only 27 amendments. Many of the most important amendments have been about the right to vote. These amendments have made it possible for more people to vote.

Some Amendments to the Constitution

Year

1791
Amendments 1 to 10
Bill of Rights

1800

1850

1865
Amendment 13
Slavery Abolished

1870
Amendment 15
African American
Men Get the Vote

1971
Amendment 26
Voting Age Lowered to 18

1900

1920
Amendment 19
Women Get the Vote

1950

2000

Write About It

In what century did African American men get the right to vote?

In 1971, the voting age was lowered from 21 to 18. How many years have passed since then?

The United States: Its People and Its Meaning

The United States means different things to different people. Here are some examples.

The promise of America is a simple promise. Every person shall share in the blessings of this land. And they shall share on the basis of their merits as a person. They shall not be judged by their color or by their beliefs or by their religion or by where they were born or the neighborhood in which they live.

Lyndon Johnson, 36th President of the United States

"E pluribus unum."
(From many, one.)

Motto of the United States of America

Write About It

Which one of these best expresses your feelings about the United States? Write something that expresses your feelings.

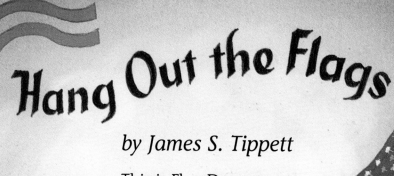

Hang Out the Flags

by James S. Tippett

This is Flag Day.
Hang out the flags;
Watch them rise with the breeze
And droop when it sags.
Hang out the flags.

Hang them from short poles;
Hang them from long.
See their bright colors
Shimmering strong,
Drifting along.

Flags mean our Homeland,
Country we love.
Let them sparkle in sunshine
Proudly above,
Showing our love.

Flags are for you,
And flags are for me.
Hang out the flags
For all men to see.
Let them hang free.

Talk About It

The feeling of love for one's country is called patriotism. Can new citizens to a country feel patriotism? Why do you think so?

Tell what you learned.

1. The U.S. government is a system of checks and balances. What does that mean?

2. If you could add an amendment to the Constitution, what would it be?

3. Which branch of the government – legislative, executive, or judicial – would you prefer to have a job in? What job would you like to do? Why?

4. The President lives in the White House, but many people say that it is the people's home. What do you think they mean by this?

Writer's Workshop

Follow these steps to be a good writer.

1 Prewriting

Choose a topic.
List your ideas about the topic.
Ask friends for ideas.
Look in books for ideas.

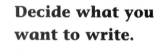

family
friends
my neighborhood
celebrations and parties
school
sports
hobbies and things I like to do
places I have visited

Decide what you want to write.
Do you want to write a story?
Do you want to explain something?
Do you want to describe something?
Do you want to tell how you feel?

Focus your topic.
Use a graphic organizer.
Focus on one idea.

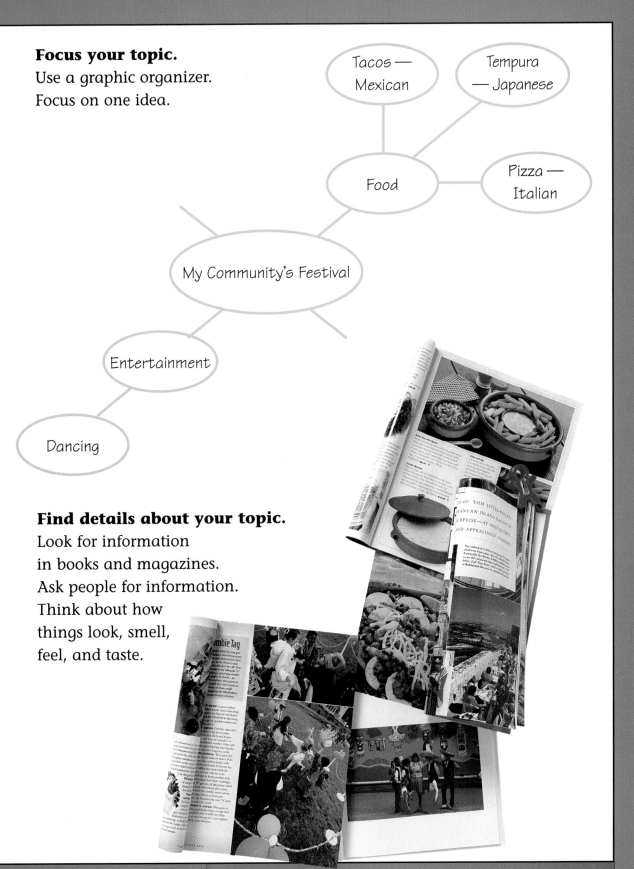

Tacos — Mexican

Tempura — Japanese

Pizza — Italian

Food

My Community's Festival

Entertainment

Dancing

Find details about your topic.
Look for information
in books and magazines.
Ask people for information.
Think about how
things look, smell,
feel, and taste.

② Drafting

Get what you need.

Get paper and pencils.

Get your graphic organizer and list of ideas.

Sit in a comfortable place.

Set a goal.

How much will you write now?

Read your notes.

What do you want to say first?

Keep writing.

Write down all your ideas. Don't worry about spelling and punctuation now.

My Community's Festival

Last sumer my community had a big festival. Restaurants in the community sold food at small stands. We ate pizza from a Italian restaurant and tacos from a Mexican restaurant. I really liked the fried vegetables called tempura from a japanese restaurant.

Dancers did dances from Ireland and Polish on a stage they wore beautiful costumes from their countries. After it gets dark, we watch fireworks.

❸ Revising

Read what you wrote. Ask yourself:
Does my story have a beginning, a middle,
and an end?
Is my information correct?
What parts should I keep?
What parts should I leave out?

I think I need a better ending.

Talk with someone.
Show your writing to a friend or your teacher.
Do your readers understand your writing?

Who are the "we" in your story?

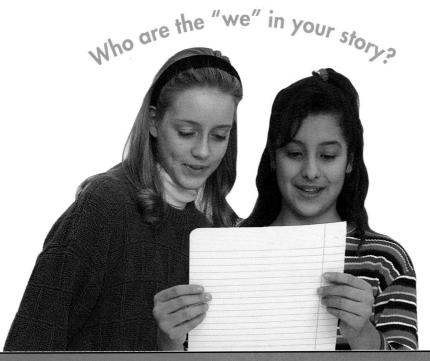

Proofreading

Check your spelling.
Look in a dictionary or ask for help.

Look for capital letters.

Look for correct punctuation.

Make a new copy.

≡	**Make a capital.**
/	**Make a small letter.**
∧	**Add something.**
ℓ	**Take out something.**
⊙	**Add a period.**
¶	**New paragraph.**

My Community's Festival

Last sumer my community had a big festival.
I went to the festival with friends from my
school. Restaurants in the community sold food
at small stands. We ate pizza from a Italian
restaurant and tacos from a Mexican
restaurant. I really liked the fried vegetables
called tempura from a japanese restaurant.
   Dancers did folk dances from Ireland and
Poland Polish on a stage they wore beautiful costumes
from their countries. After it gets dark, we
watch fireworks. I want to go to the festival
again next summer so I can taste more foods.
I can't wait!

⑤ Presenting

Share your writing.
Read it aloud to your family or classmates.
Make a book. Lend the book to your family
or classmates.

My Community's Festival

Last summer my community had a big festival.
I went to the festival with friends from my school.
Restaurants in the community sold food at small
stands. We ate pizza from an Italian restaurant
and tacos from a Mexican restaurant. I really
liked the fried vegetables called tempura from
a Japanese restaurant.

Dancers did folk dances from Ireland and
Poland on a stage. They wore beautiful costumes
from their countries. After it got dark,
we watched fireworks.

I want to go to the festival again next summer
so I can taste more foods. I can't wait!

What a Good Writer Can Do

- I plan before I write.

- I can write about things I know. I can write about my family, my school, and myself.

- I can write stories with a beginning, a middle, and an end.

- I can ask others to read my work.

- I can write in complete sentences.

- I can put periods at the end of sentences.

- I can make my handwriting easy to read.